A RUN TO THE

RIVER

A RUN TO THE RIVER

RON GLODICH

PRAISE FOR

A RUN TO THE RIVER

A Run to the River is a book that will resonate with every coach and his or her unfailing drive to lift and inspire an entire community as together they support the growth of their student athletes into fine men and women. EVERY town needs a Ron Glodich.

~ Jarvis Johnson, Former National Football League (NFL) player, Coach, and philanthropist

Anyone who meets Ron Glodich, in person, or through this book, becomes a fan. One of the finest educators and coaches I was privileged to work with in my 39 years in public education, Ron understands team culture, as highlighted in this book. His creative coaching and strong relationship with his players led to his tremendous success—including a state championship and Hall of Fame induction—as documented in his new adventure in life, as an author. If you love underdog sports stories, this book is a must read.

~ David Scheel, Retired School Counselor, Retired Stadium Announcer

Excelling at one thing in life is rare. Now retired from coaching, Ron Glodich's unprecedented and significant record speaks for his excellence on the field. As an author, his storytelling shows his next chapter of accolades."

"Commitment and character, as the battle cry of Coach Ron, leads this incredible team, as well as the book's readers, to fields of greatness and lessons worth celebrating."

"Ron Glodich is the coach every parent wishes their student athlete had. An engaging memoir, *A Run to the River* is equally entertaining as the reader experiences Friday Night Lights, Marine City style, and revels in its unique traditions. One can easily see why sports is at the heart of this idyllic town."

A RUN TO THE

BY

RON GLODICH

SILVERLIGHT PRESS

P.O. Box 342544,
Austin, Texas 78734

https://www.throughpenandlens.com/

*To the small group of women who truly
understand the coach's grind:*

*Katherine Glodich,
Debbie Staskiewicz,
and
Melisa Scarcelli.*

*To my father, who created the strongest
pillars for my success, both in life and football,
from his heart, work ethic, and values.*

*I love you, Dad. I miss you more than you can
imagine. Here's to you…just checking in!*

"Who's the man with the
big blue nose?
Ooh ahh ooh ahh.

We will run the ball till
we break their bones!

Ooh ahh ooh ahh.

We will not stop till we
drop dead!
Ooh ahh ooh ahh.

Who are, who are,
who are we?

We are the boys from
Marine City!

Ooh ahh ooh ahh—
Yeaaah!

~ Newton-King

New Zealand foreign exchange

Class of 1990, and Creator of our traditional post-game

victory chant beginning 1989.

CONTENTS

FOREWORD

I FIRST MET Ron Glodich when I interviewed him for a Science Teacher opening in 1987. He came across as intelligent and thoughtful, and more important—meticulous. There was an exactness and detail I had never seen before, in the way he spoke and presented himself—something you wouldn't see in most football coaches. He had great conversation skills and was an even better listener. He was a perfectionist who strived to offer the best to others. His unique and colorful personality was infectious and most likely why he became so successful. By the end of that interview there wasn't a doubt in my mind he would be a Mariner, and in true Ron Glodich fashion, he told me exactly that.

Before I met Ron, I coached the varsity football program at Marine City High School for over 12 years, then changed course and became the Athletic Director. During those years of coaching, I did my best to establish and construct a program to be respected and aspirational. One instilled with commitment, discipline, and community support. When hiring the next round of coaches, I had a strong opinion about who I wanted. The Mariners needed coaches with more knowledge, creativeness, and thirst to take the program further. And I knew digging in would be worth it in the end.

A Run to the River provides the reader with more than an accounting of how a small-town football program operates. It also dives into the relationships born from the love of football and the trials and tribulations it takes to become successful. Coach Glodich's words give us hope that the history and traditions will be carried on for future generations.

ONCE A MARINER, ALWAYS A MARINER.

~ Gerald W. Warkentien
Marine City Student Athlete 1961-65
Eastern Michigan Football Player 1967-70
Head Football Coach, Marine City High School 1973-85
State Semifinalist 1985
Marine City Athletic Director 1986-2014

PREFACE

IT WAS A running joke for many during my coaching career. My common phrase was, "that's going in the book." I had talked often about writing a book relating my coaching experiences at Marine City High School once I retired from teaching. In November 2021, I contacted Susan Sember, who was a decorated and very distinguished alumni from my alma mater, Warren Fitzgerald High School. Susan had a long career in film making and was also working with authors and screenwriters in her publishing company. She invited me to be one of her selected authors and my continual statement of "that's going in the book" became reality.

A Run to the River explores the evolution of football at Marine City High School. I experienced firsthand and detail the State Championship run of the 2013 team. The initial chapters were written as I spent twelve days in my son's former bedroom and isolated with a COVID infection.

The process has been a blast as I have reconnected with several former players to get their perspective on the legendary 2013 season. Speaking with former coaches, school personnel, and community members also filled my literary bucket with interesting facts to share in the book. I look forward to sharing that journey with readers...thankful for the opportunity Susan created for me.

ACKNOWLEDGMENTS

"Show me the money!"

WRITING A BOOK and getting it published requires a significant financial investment, and without the support of my wife, Kathy Glodich, this book would not have come to life. Her magical combination of one part inspiration and one part motivation kept me on task with support and encouragement, but also, she was not afraid to give me tough love when needed. I am blessed.

My twins, Gunnar and Gabbi, continue to amaze me with the growth experienced in their professional careers and with their families; this inspired me to create something they can one day show their children with pride.

My incredibly supportive parents never missed a game and made sure I understood the balance needed between academics and athletics and gave equal praise to both endeavors.

I am also blessed to have connected with my inspiring publisher, Susan Sember, whose professional resume elevates her to a level that few can match. When she shared some positive comments about my writing style, it was as if a shot of adrenaline was injected into my body. Her publishing team on my project, which included Anna Weber, Randy Goad, Laura Picarelli, and Matt Dodge helped me construct something worthy of being published.

My best friend and cousin, Mark Gorski, and his wife Candi, became intellectual venting posts during the many vacations we shared. Whether it was around a campfire or a kitchen table playing Euchre, their insight into my skill set and thoughts about publishing helped to cement the decision.

Fellow coaches and mentors Bob Staskiewicz, Tony Scarcelli, and Jerry Warkentien help me recreate a long career of memories that were inspiration for the book. Meetings with Tim McConnell, Andy Scheel, Dave Frendt, and Dave Scheel fed me with historical information to make the book authentic.

Finally, my brothers, Jim and John Glodich, created an atmosphere in which I grew up that showed the positive benefits of hard work, competition, and evaluation. I have said many times that my love of sports and coaching comes directly from my family—and any success I achieved resulted directly from two great older brothers.

INTRODUCTION

HAVE YOU EVER tried to accomplish something big but could never get over the hump and pull in that ultimate prize? Would you be willing to keep trying for 10 years? The Marine City football program lost to local rival, Marysville, 10 straight times from the years 1986 to 1996, but ultimately climbed a proverbial hill to the summit and stayed on top.

Demonstrations of maximum performance and teamwork, added to the success of our program and were woven through the Mariner's fiber. Our grit, determination, endurance, and unity won the heart of the Marine City community. As an assistant coach, I had a front-row seat for much of the ride, and eventually became the head coach of this amazing program. The ride helped to mold me into the coach and person I am today.

The ride was not always smooth, the crowd was not always friendly, and this coach was not always sane in his approach. It is my hope, however, by reading these stories the end result will cause your heart to swell, your blood pressure to rise, and a tear to form in your eye. Enjoy this crazy ride that ends in the river of this beautiful town.

Go Black!

A RUN TO THE RIVER| Ron Glodich

A RUN TO THE

RIVER

1

REDEMPTION.

THE PARENTAL BUZZARDS hovered in the air. They could smell the fresh meat and were looking to scavenge. Like a virus spreading, the noise started in the community with only a few, but as the season drew closer, the population grew, and so did the negative noise. Faith in the Mariner's program was being questioned. Opposing coaches were giddy and spouted off the idea that the Marine City Mariners' successful run was over.

The Marine City High School football program had become one of the top programs in Michigan. This bedroom community sits northeast of Detroit and is nestled on the St. Clair River, which separates the eastern edge of Michigan's thumb from its international neighbor, Canada. Going into the 2013 season, the Mariners had qualified for the state playoffs for 15 consecutive years. They were in the midst of 30 straight winning seasons, experienced their ,historic first state championship in 2007 and rallied for a state runner-up finish in 2011. But in 2012 a new head coach took over the program, and they went 8-2 in his inaugural season. For most fans, that type of season would be a great launching pad, but the Mariners lost twice in the same year to local rival Richmond and the team was knocked out of the playoffs in the first round. The last time Marine City was knocked out that early was in 1998. For the Mariner faithful, 8-2 and an early playoff exit was nothing short of disappointing.

I was the new head coach and replaced Tony Scarcelli, who retired as a member of the Michigan high school football coach's hall of fame. For several years, Tony and I were coordinators for Bob Staskiewicz. Tony was on the defensive side, and I was the Mariners' offensive coordinator. Coach Bob was also in the Hall of Fame and came to Marine City the same year I did, in 1987. Coach Bob was the ideal head coach to work under as he strategically gave each of us more ownership on our side of the ball. Through Coach Bob's vision and the support of the wonderful Athletic Director, Jerry Warkentien, the Mariner football program started its momentum. Coach Bob retired in 2004 when Tony took the reins and maintained the duties until he retired in 2011. Several members of our coaching staff, including Matt Pollock and Daryn Letson, remained, and I felt we still had the best staff in the area.

To add to the drama of the 2013 season, the Mariner's opening game was against long-time rival Richmond—at Richmond. The 2012 team was light on seniors, so we returned many of our starters going into 2013. The major change was in our quarterback—where we started Alex

Merchant, a transfer from Port Huron Northern. His family had purchased a funeral parlor in town and made a full residence change. Years later, Alex revealed to me that he had not been enthusiastic about the transfer because he had outstanding success in his sophomore year at PHN (a spread offense team). Alex would replace Jarrett Mathison, who had an extraordinarily successful sophomore season as our quarterback.

The community was not in support of this change, and it helped fuel the growing noise. Jarrett's parents were not happy with the change and encouraged him to have a one-on-one meeting with me. Jarrett and I had a great relationship and the last thing I wanted to do was to cheat him out of any goals or aspirations he had. I laid out to this valued athlete what I felt his new role would be and how deeply I believed this change could lead to some great things for our team. So, it was born—the idea of TEAM OVER TALENT—which sprang from Jarrett Mathison's willingness to set aside his personal objectives to be the Mariner quarterback...and do what was best for the team.

August 30, 2013, was a beautiful summer night for football. The smell of fresh cut grass was mixed with the tantalizing smells from the concession stand, offset by the beautiful colors of a sunset you can only see in Michigan. Sounds flooded the night air from the band's drum section...to the cheerleaders' practice routines...to the rhythmic chants of the player warmups. The Mariner fans showed up early to grab spots in the small visitor section at Richmond stadium. In the corner of the stands stood the group of dads who historically became very vocal during the game. They became the loudest when the Mariners were at their worst. Their behavior embarrassed many loyal fans, and the rowdy dad section took on a black hole phenomenon because people avoided it at all costs—lest they get sucked into the insanity. The testosterone was pervasive, but numerous fans could create a buffer between themselves and the madness. The stands filled up quickly and the overflow crowd lined the fence, circling the field. Packed bleachers and a crowded fence line created an amazing environment for our young men and for high school football. One thing I always tried to stress to our teams before big games was to step back and enjoy the environment.

I stressed to them...transfer your fear and anxiety to thankfulness and appreciation that your team can be involved in such a great night.

The Mariners scored on their opening drive with a tight end seam pass to gifted athlete, Pete Patsalis, who was a captain and a two-way player with ideal leadership skills. Pete oozed positivity but was not afraid to challenge his teammates when needed. A relentless worker, he was also the catalyst for one of the greatest offseason programs we had ever experienced. Pete was a sophomore starter on our 2011 state runner-up team, and he seemed driven to get his team back to Ford Field. The touchdown pass from Alex to Pete immediately squelched many critics' questions about Alex as the quarterback. For the extra point, we brought out junior, Miss Olivia Viney. Olivia's dad was our soccer coach, and he worked with Olivia all summer to improve her timing and distance. She kicked successfully for our JV team in 2012, but this would be her first varsity game and her first varsity attempt.

From the snapper, Josh Albo, to holder, Jarrett Mathison, the ball set perfectly for Olivia. This was another major contention with the community. "How can he let a girl kick for us?" was a frequent question. Olivia aggressively attacked the ball on the tee and her first varsity extra point attempt went down the middle of the uprights. Our team embraced her, protected her, and knew she would be a weapon for us.

Why did I allow Olivia to kick?

She was the best we had!

Richmond answered on their first offensive play with an 85-yard bomb down the Richmond sideline, and with their college-bound kicker, they made the score 7-7. Although we scored on our first drive, we seemed slow and out of sync with our next few possessions. Richmond tacked on a field goal and after a Mariner fumble, added another touchdown in the second quarter to take a 17-7 lead. Flashbacks to the 2012 games immediately rushed into my head. In game one, we relinquished an 11-point lead in the fourth quarter and lost 25-24, and in game two, we missed a field goal late in the game to lose 21-24. With doubt setting in on the Mariner sideline, the mob squad of dads in the corner of the bleachers ramped up their vocal barrage like never before. This type of adult behavior is simply one of the ugliest things to occur in an otherwise amazing environment. Their words never pierced my presence as the double-eared headphones block out all noise pollution, but I wondered, *do these dads realize the effect they might have on the players?*

In our next possession, we hit Jarrett Mathison out of the backfield on a wheel route, where he outraced Richmond defenders for an 87-yard touchdown pass. Jarrett and I joke every time we see each other about how he drove me crazy in practice because he never went 100%. He was what in the coaching profession we call a *gamer*. The things Jarrett would do in a game were never seen on the practice field. He became a different person on game day, and on this touchdown, he displayed speed I had never seen from him. It was a touchdown that was the turning point for our team. The players now understood our power was with Alex as our quarterback, a deep ball threat in Pete, an explosive running back in Jarrett, and an offensive line that lived in the weight room. We now had the tools to score. Olivia was again perfect on her extra point, and we trailed 17-14 with just five minutes left in the first half.

The Mariner defense locked in and forced a Richmond punt after just three plays. Corner, Grant Sharpe, attacked a sweep play and tackled the Richmond running back for a loss of three yards on first down and Captain, Alec Adams, collapsed the offensive line and forced a no gain on second-down. A shanked punt followed a failed third-down pass attempt. Marine City took over on the Richmond 38-yard line.

Our first down offensive coordinator, Daryn Letson, called for a PLAY ACTION PASS and Pete Patsalis ran a textbook seam route—Alex connected again for a big gain to the seven-yard line. Jarrett scored two plays later and Olivia converted a line drive just barely clearing the cross bar. The Mariners were back on top 21-17 with just two minutes left in the half.

As quickly as our confidence grew, it was deflated with a 35-yard fade pass for a Richmond touchdown...with just 15 seconds left in the half. The extra point was good—the Richmond Blue Devils went into their locker room at halftime with a 24-21 lead over the Mariners. We took our team to the south end zone and gathered for our halftime adjustments. This was our normal practice with away games as I tried to avoid our players having to mix with visiting crowds. Unfortunately for us, the vocal dad group let the coaching staff have it and screamed their displeasure from the fence line. I was always amazed by some of these same dads who would come up after a winning game to shake my hand and say, "Good job." Matt Pollock, our defensive coach, made his adjustments, and Daryn Letson, our offensive coordinator, did the same. Both coaches displayed calm and focus.

Our kids were playing their hearts out and there was no need to adjust their effort.

I reiterated to the kids, "we knew it would be another four-quarter war like the games in 2012." Richmond had an outstanding wrestling program, and you could see early in the game that their physicality was getting the better of us. I felt our kids were making great adjustments as the game progressed with pad level and foot movement. I challenged them to stay with our plan through the fourth quarter and let our offseason conditioning program lead us into victory.

Richmond kicked off to us to open the second half. The Mariners use a special kickoff return I brought to MC in 1988—called the STARBURST. It is simply four backs converging quickly and carrying out fakes in all different directions. The Mariners are known statewide for the success we've long had with this return. In all their previous kicks to us, Richmond angled kicks short, to avoid this return. On this particular kick, they errored and kicked it deep into one of our backs. Pete Patsalis received the ball in a multi-fake mixer and raced 91 yards for a touchdown. Olivia was good on the kick and the Mariners regained the lead in this crazy back-and-forth game, 28-24.

Just minutes later, Richmond raced 55 yards on an off-tackle play to retake the lead (Richmond 31—MC 28). We answered with passes to Pete and rushes from Jarrett to go back on top (MC 35—Richmond 31) to end the third quarter. Early in the fourth quarter, Richmond hit yet another fade route on their sideline to make it Richmond 38—MC 35. With about six minutes to go in the game, the Mariners had the ball at midfield and attempted a dive off the right side to Jarrett Mathison. He was met behind the line of scrimmage by two Richmond defenders and his progress was stopped. But he spun out, found a gap, and raced 10 yards for the first down. As

Jarrett emerged from the pile, he nodded his head up and down again and again. It was as if he was saying to himself and to our team, "They can't stop me, they can't stop me." It was an injection of energy felt on the field and on our sideline. The swell of energy became contagious to our fans, and the noise that followed provided pure adrenaline for our mission. On the next play, Jarrett took the ball on a fullback trap, bounced off a linebacker, and raced 45 yards for the next Mariner touchdown. Again, Jarret sprinted through two Richmond defenders with a speed we had never witnessed before. With Jarrett making huge plays as a defensive back for us and scoring touchdowns late in the game, moving Alex to quarterback and Jarrett to two-way player seemed to be the right one. The Mariners were back on top late in the game MC 42—Richmond 38.

The game proceeded with a failed offensive series from both teams (three and outs) and as time closed in on the two-minute mark remaining, Richmond had the ball on their own 10-yard line. Richmond had an outstanding quarterback who would go on to play in college, a great wideout with exceptional speed, a big tight end with great hands, and a powerful running back. Although we had given up 38 points, I felt our defense was strengthening as the game progressed and we were getting progressively better. The Mariner defense had a couple of sophomore starters, and you could see them gaining confidence as the game moved on. Richmond utilized all their weapons, put together a beautiful two-minute drill, and got the ball down to the Mariner three-yard line with just 25 seconds remaining. With no timeouts remaining, the Blue Devils attempted a quarterback sneak on the next play and sophomore linebacker, Dennis Fitzsimmons ducked under a blocker, stood up the quarterback, and drove him backwards for a loss of yardage. With nine seconds remaining, the Blue Devils quickly assembled and spiked the ball to stop the clock. The stadium noise grew in anticipation of the last play of the game. Not one person in that stadium was seated. Everyone was up on their feet, screaming at the top of their lungs. Richmond took the snap and ran a stretch play to their sideline. The running back had a full head of steam, and with blockers out in front, dove for the goal line pylon. A host of Mariners, led by Pete Patsalis and Jarrett Mathison, met him, deflected his momentum out of bounds and prevented him from scoring.

The sideline official waved his arms back and forth across his body to signal no score and the Mariners rushed the field from the sideline. In the middle of the celebration noise and hugs, we heard the whistle blowing repeatedly. The lead official made his way over to me and stated, "Coach, there is still one second left on the clock." What we learned later is that as the officials headed off the field, the Richmond Athletic Director grabbed them to say there was still time on the clock. That's not his job, and to this day I don't know why the official even let it come into play. I began a long conversation with the official, forcing him to explain how time remained. Matt Pollock, our defensive coordinator, seized the opportunity and quickly got our defense organized and ready for the *next last play* of the game. I don't believe the Richmond staff did the same because I noticed their kids meandering on the sideline. After the dust settled, we resumed the action to run the final play of the game—once again. The ball was spotted on the right hash and on the one-yard line. Coach Pollock had inserted Kenton Rivard at nose guard. Kenton was 6-2 and 300 pounds and one of our strongest kids. Coach Pollock instructed him to get under the center and drive him back with as much force as he could. Kenton was instructed to forget about tackling anyone and to just drive the center back.

Richmond promptly snapped the ball and attempted a quarterback sneak. The quarterback immediately stood up as Kenton drove the center back into the quarterback. A stalemate occurred, and defensive end, Alex Adams, came off the edge, grabbed the quarterback, and pulled him back and down. The Mariners withstood two goal-line attempts, rushed the field a second time, and walked away with one of the hardest-fought victories they had ever experienced.

As for the dads in the corner of the stands...it has been verified multiple times by multiple observers that one dad became so enraged after the first goal-line attempt he barfed over the top railing onto the surrounding cement. I later responded to a local reporter saying, "Our fans *are* something!"

2

THE GRIND.

THE ALARM CLOCK rang at 5:15 a.m. and I did my best to shut it down quickly. Moving as quietly as a cat burglar, I got ready while trying not to wake my wife, Kathy. I poured some coffee, headed out the door, and slid into the Durango at 5:50 a.m. A quick right, a left, and one more right and I was driving down the long street that made up the waterfront in downtown Marine City. The street was dark and empty until I parked my car in front of Paul's Bakery.

Danielle opened the front door at 6:00 a.m. and I entered immediately. She had my preordered donuts waiting on the counter and we had a nice, quick conversation. Knowing what the donuts were for, she always gave us a Mariner discount. I exited the store and enjoyed one of my favorite personal rituals. The peace and tranquility of the waterfront downtown in the early morning resembled a Hallmark card, so I purposely stopped and smelled the air. There was no snow on

15

the ground on this February morning, so the streetlights bounced off the store fronts and created a warming glow. Looking to my left and then to my right, I saw no cars, I saw no movement...I just saw calmness. That, matched with the smell of brisk winter air mixed with the unique smell of the river, created an aroma that made for an amazing start for my day.

I was then off to Marine City High School, where I parked in my usual spot, right next to my classroom in the west teachers' lot. There were no other cars in the pitch-black parking lot as I gathered my duffle bag and the donuts and headed inside. It was February 4, 2013, and this was the first day of DAWN PATROL, which was a tradition that Coach Bob started in the early 90s as a way of getting his offensive lineman to move better. It started with roughly a dozen linemen who came in to play dodgeball in our small auxiliary gym.

I gathered my whistle, my drill script, and the donuts and headed toward the gym. The athletes entered the east side of the building, so I never knew how many were present until I entered the gym. Approaching the room, I peered into the small rectangular window in the gym door. Standing in front of the stage on the south end of the basketball court were roughly 60 Mariners waiting for this morning's workout. Dawn Patrol had developed into a speed and agility workout and all football players from all levels were invited.

I am a science teacher by profession, and although I don't consider myself a rah-rah, high-energy type of guy, I love to observe interactions. It was 6:15 a.m. with Dawn Patrol set to

16

start at 6:25 a.m., which provided me with 10 minutes of observations. Most players did not realize I was watching them as I covertly pretended to be busy at mid-court, setting up the gym's sound system. Some were sitting on the stage as if they were drugged with the most potent cough medicine. A few were wide awake and collecting into small gossip groups. And then, there were those who were more conservative and quieter, who migrated to the opposite end, away from the gossip group. There were also a few loners who wanted nothing to do with anybody at that time of day.

Dawn Patrol to me was an early indicator of a team's dynamics and commitment. It was voluntary and if an athlete made it to all eight sessions in February, they were rewarded with the coveted simple T-shirt that broadcasted their success and commitment. Unintentionally, the team's leaders were exposed when I asked the seniors to set up a long turf mat on the gym floor. The turf mat was heavy and on a couple of rollers stored in the auxiliary gym. The journey from there to the main gym was paved with some tight turns, which meant teamwork and precision driving were needed. How smoothly the players made the journey and how neatly they rolled the mat out onto the floor spoke to their leadership skills.

"Early is on time and on time is late," was a saying I heard at a coaching clinic and stole to use frequently with our players. The Marine City athletes had it drilled in their heads and would hold each other accountable if they were late or tardy. I made eye contact with Pete Patsalis, who was designated to be one of our captains for 2013, and he knew it was time to start Dawn Patrol. Pete quickly organized the group into lines and started our agility warmups. Wanna-be captains jumped to the front of the lines and jockeyed for position for the remaining three captain spots.

After the agility warmups, Pete organized the group into stretch lines. Each line captain would announce the stretch and would count out the beats. This is where I enjoyed moving through the lines and commenting to the groggy athletes. "Glad to see you combed your hair this morning, Kenton." "What did you have for breakfast, Ethan?" "Damn, Kevin, are you wearing Garanimals, because that is one sweet outfit."

"Coach, what are Garanimals?" he responded.

"Study your history," I barked back.

I would also have some good ole fashion eighties rock and roll on the loudspeakers and would ask athletes, "Who is this artist?" Occasionally, I would get the right answer from someone who had parents that enjoyed the same music. On most Dawn Patrol mornings, other coaches would attend. I was lucky enough to be just five minutes from the school, but Coach Frendt and Coach Scheel were a good 30 minutes out, and to use this time to get a look at the younger athletes meant their morning started early.

We may not have realized it, but the interactions between the coaches modeled an atmosphere for optimal performance. We were upbeat, friendly, and cared deeply about each other. No one was immune to some light kidding, including me, and we often laughed through the entire workout. But we also realized how important these workouts were to establish the tone for the year.

To keep things fresh, we would vary the speed and agility drills for each session, but we always liked to finish the workouts with short 25-yard sprints and celebrate the winner. This reflected a competitive spirit, willingness to be challenged, and of course, the speed of an athlete. Much to our surprise was the realization that a couple of our big linemen were moving much better than last year, and this was a credit for their dedication in the weight room.

We ended the first Dawn Patrol at 7:10 a.m., which gave the athletes 15 minutes to get ready for first-hour class. Donuts were passed out to the coaches and the 60-plus athletes in attendance. I filmed some of the workout and posted it on to the Mariners' Facebook page and comments flooded in— encouraging the Mariners and supporting Coach Bob's tradition.

With my favorite donut in hand, I headed back to my classroom to take on the day. If I passed an athlete that didn't make it to Dawn Patrol, I would simply say, "Morning, Bobby, we missed you this morning." I would follow up later in the day to make sure everything was ok. One thing I learned early in coaching is that you never know what is going on in the home life of a student athlete.

3

THE FORMULA.

ENTERING THE 2013 season, the Mariner football program had some amazing success, and the foundation was built on the shoulders of two great visionaries, one of whom was Jerry Warkentien, a three-sport athlete who attended Marine City High School and played college baseball and football at Eastern Michigan University. He ultimately returned to Marine City to become the program's head coach in 1973. Jerry fixed the messy program and improved low numbers. The Mariners played their games right at the high school in a field that was a short walk across the parking lot.

In the seventies, rowdy town locals and poor field lighting made for a sketchy, alcohol-fueled atmosphere. In 1975, the rotting wooden light poles surrounding the field were finally cut down. Then the administration hosted home games at 4:00 p.m. to make the atmosphere more family friendly. Jerry's greatest accomplishment came in rebuilding the sports program after budget cuts decimated athletics and caused the district to drop fall sports entirely in 1979. Many of the Mariners' top athletes transferred out of the school and most did not return the following year when football was reinstated. Following a full year without sports, Coach Warkentien, helped by longtime assistant Bill Ameel, inspired the Mariner's renewed football momentum.

The program's consecutive winning seasons stretched to thirty years as we rolled into the 2013 season with a win streak started in 1983 with Coach Warkentien going 6-3 that year. He followed with another 6-3 year in 1984 and then finished his coaching reign with a league championship and a Class B semifinal appearance in 1985. The Mariners finished 10-2 that season, making it the greatest season in Mariner history.

Another historic event in 1985 was the Mariners' first victory over the area's perennial powerhouse and football giant...the Marysville Vikings. This team was the golden standard for all football programs in the entire state. They had a legendary Hall of fame coach in Walt Braun, who was able to assemble a staff that stayed together for many years, which included defensive coordinator, Jim Venia. This consistency of coaches at every level seemed to be the blueprint for high school football success. Jerry transitioned from head football coach to assistant principal/athletic director and looked to hire a new head coach. It was the Mariner basketball coach at the time (Daryl Walker) who threw out the name of his *good buddy* from the Port Sanilac area, Bob Staskiewicz. Bob, the head coach at Deckerville, a small school situated in the thumb of Michigan, had a nice run of success there between 1977-

1986. He and I were hired in 1987 by Jerry Warkentien—with Bob as head coach. I assumed the defensive coordinator job on the JV, working with Coach Larry Rombach. Coach Rombach was the perfect guy to start my career with because he made things so fun and interesting. Larry would be scout team QB (mimicking the other team's quarterback in scrimmage time) and run right at the players even though he wore no pads. If I blew the whistle early, he would growl, "Don't blow the whistle until they drag me down!"

What was immediately established with our teaching placement was COACHES IN THE BUILDING, and anyone who has ever coached at the high school level realizes there is no better catalyst for energy in a program than to have kids constantly see a coach in the building. Bob inherited Tony Scarcelli, who was a towering young model of Italian athleticism, as his defensive coordinator. He started at Marine City in 1986 but will be the first to tell you he was not ready to be a head coach at that time. Tony was a Warren Woods High School graduate who won a state championship there in 1978. I was familiar with Tony since Warren Woods was the archrival of my high school, Warren Fitzgerald. I had also witnessed him play when I was a freshman in high school. In 1978 when Tony won state, Fitzgerald had them on the ropes in Game 9 of that year and could have knocked them out of the playoffs, but Tony's Warriors pulled out the win on the final play of the game.

Coach Bob and Coach Scar were both gym teachers who directly recruited and made sure our best athletes would play football. Coach Bob physically looked like anything but a head football coach. He was just a little over 5-7, with dirty blond hair, and our kids thought he resembled Gilligan on the old 70s sitcom, *Gilligan's Island.* He had the piercing blue eyes and leathery tan of an outdoorsman. He never wore a hat, walked with a little duck foot, and when he ran, his arms were pulled into his body way too tight. But boy could he bellow! When he let the vocal cords fly, his voice could be heard well across the gym or practice field. Tony, on the other hand, stood 6-4, and sported thick curly Italian hair and a porn star mustache. He played college football at the University of Illinois and still looked the part as he transitioned into teaching. The girls at Marine City High School were drawn to this young teacher, and Tony and I were both single at the time, so it made things interesting. When Coach Bob and Coach Scar stood side by side, it was an amazing contrast of styles—both physically and in the way they treated kids. The bottom line was that their ability to connect with kids was amazingly effective and anytime you ask a former Mariner, they will tell you the same thing.

It was a two-headed system, where kids were constantly challenged to get involved. Tony had an amazing sense of humor where he essentially was *ripping on* kids, yet they enjoyed it and would come back for more. "Hey Jimmy, what is that string hanging off your shoulder? Oh, sorry, that's your arm," was one of his favorite rips. He had a great nick name system and once he hung one on you, it would stay with you for your entire high school career. *Mayor McCheese, Beef,* and *Action Jackson* were some of his best.

Coach Bob was a conversationalist and would engage kids in their likes, hobbies, and families, and would connect well with kids from every background. A history buff and a superb storyteller, the kids always enjoyed the back-and-forth banter Coach Bob often supplied.

What quickly evolved because the coaching staff worked so closely together in the building was a community that expanded to include our wives and children, and where a great deal of time was spent together. The families held after-game parties...with each family taking a turn. We ate lunch together, often shared dinner and movies on the weekend, and we sometimes vacationed together. In becoming close friends, our commitment to the success of the program intensified as our friendships grew stronger.

I was blessed to develop a wonderful relationship with Coach Bob. He was 13 years older and became a mentor who was easy to talk to about anything. I respected his opinion on many things, and to this day I tell people, " I never once got a bad piece of advice from Bob Staskiewicz." As my confidence grew in coaching and teaching, my ability to tease and piss off Coach Bob grew in direct proportion. For example, Bob was what I coined an *all-or-nothing drinker* and when he *got going,* was when I had the most fun with him.

We were on spring break in 1991 and the weather that week was warm enough for us to play golf. Coach Bob, some other coaches, and I got together and headed to the Oak Ridge golf course at I-94 and 26-Mile. The exit off Interstate I-94 traveling to Marine City was roughly 15 straight miles of black top headed east into town. Anytime you headed out of Marine City, you knew it was approximately a half hour drive to get to civilization. We enjoyed our round of golf and went into the club house for a late lunch, or early dinner. A pitcher of beer was ordered and as always, we talked about football and how to improve the program. That was one of Coach Bob's strengths—he was an expert in engaging his coaches in conversations and drawing their insights into the open. He valued the opinions he received and constantly asked, "What do you think about this?" On this particular night, the discussion centered on our regional championship loss to Dearborn Robichaud and their U of M, NFL-bound star, Tyronne Wheatley, was at the forefront. It was an emotional game, one in which we held the lead until the middle of the fourth quarter.

Our 1990 team was a talented team led by quarterback, Rob Tenyer, who, at the time of publishing *Run for the River*, is the head football coach at Morehead State University. Linemen, Frank Clemente, Mike Tranchida, and Jimmy Schuster blocked for talented running backs: John Griffor, Jim Heaslip, and Dave Walker.

I tell people we had the lead in that game until we pissed off Tyrone! He was the best high school player I ever witnessed, and to this day, that holds true. More beer was ordered, the intensity of the conversation grew, and Coach Bob transitioned into his alter state of *all-or-nothing drinker*. He would order rounds whether you wanted one or not, and if you declined, he would make insinuating comments about your manhood. He had an amazing technique when you waffled on a drinking decision. "Well then, let's split one," he would offer. Before you knew it, you had split three beers with the man.

As we drove back into town and stopped at the high school to drop each other off, Coach Bob was determined to have one more drink at a local bar downtown called Gords, an old-school, no-frills bar. It had a big wooden bar near the entrance and a couple tables that hugged the opposing wall; it transitioned into a couple of pool tables and then a long, thin tabletop shuffleboard game. The building was long and narrow, with an opening that faced the St. Clair River, so anyone sitting at the bar had a nice waterfront view.

I was recently married and had no interest in hitting another bar and was, quite frankly...ready to go home. I was the polar opposite of Coach Bob where, once I started drinking, I had a three-hour window and was ready for bed. It was well beyond three hours, so I was done for the night. Coach Bob insisted I come with him for one more drink. I insisted I was done! As I exited his van, I noticed Coach Bob exit from the driver's seat, and heard him bark, "I am going to ask you one more time. Are you going to Gords with me?" I also noticed the *insane* look in his eyes and realized he was clearly still reeling from the earlier conversation about our regional loss to Robichaud. His jaw was clenched, and I swore I saw smoke come from his nose! Coach Bob had long been known as an intense competitor, and it spilled out into this night. He was determined to continue talking about ways to improve Mariner Football. I chose not to look at him and lifted my golf clubs over my shoulder. As I lifted them, my ribs were exposed, and Coach Bob delivered an upward solar punch to my rib section. It took me by complete surprise, and I burst out laughing. It reminded me of the Woody Hayes undercut punch to a Clemson ball carrier on the sideline in Woody's last year. Ironically, Woody Hayes was Coach Bob's idol, so maybe there was a spiritual connection that night. As Coach Bob got in his van and sped off, I laughed and as I limped to my car, asked myself, "Did that really just happen?" I could not stop laughing and when I walked into my house, I had a smirk on my face that made my wife ask, "What the hell happened to you?"

THE PROCESS.

WHEN MOST PEOPLE venture out to Marine City High School from the Detroit area, they travel east and north on Interstate 94 until they reach Exit 248—the Marine City Highway. They make a right turn and head down 12 miles of straight two-lane highway until it ends at King Road. A right turn on King Road and within two miles is the high school. North of Marine City lays a township called East China—named after the China clay commonly found in the soil. East China School district contains two high schools that are anchored in two distinctly different communities. To the south is the waterfront town of Marine City and up the St. Clair River lies another waterfront town, St. Clair. Marine City High School and St. Clair High School are the two dominant players in the East China School District.

After the Richmond game season opener in 2013, we prepared for our first home game. Marine City football home games had become a community-wide extravaganza that incorporated a huge sample of the students in the high school. In my second year as head coach, I learned to embrace this atmosphere better and made the event one of which the community could be proud.

THE BOAT

In 1988 the district built a multimillion-dollar stadium that would be used by both high schools. The stadium was built on Meisner Road, which was roughly halfway between the two towns. In that same year Coach Bob had the idea to put a pirate ship at the stadium, paint it black, and hoist flags with skulls and cross bones into the wind. He also purchased a small working cannon and blank shells, with the idea that the cannon would blow every time the Mariners scored in a game. What resulted was a noble tradition at home games where JV players were rotated to wave enormous flags with skull and cross bones and other players sat proudly on the boat poised to blow off the cannon whenever the Mariners scored. I would always get a kick every time we played a team for the first time—seeing their reaction when the cannon blew out of the boat in the south end zone. One would see 40-50 heads snapping and turning in the same direction, usually followed by quick ducks, and hands raised toward their ears to avoid the noise.

Coach Bob explained he saw the abandoned boat in one of the corn fields that was adjacent to 26-Mile Road. He asked around in town who the owner might be, and the buzz quickly circulated. The boat was owned by the local Knights of Columbus who abandoned it after the vessel was damaged in a parade. Parent volunteers from the Richard Clemente family and the Tranchida family assembled a team and moved the boat to the Clemente residence for the transformation. Brown-stained wood was painted black, platforms for students to stand on were constructed, and tall masks carrying skulls and cross bone flags were hoisted.

The boat has gone through many transformations since then and in 2013 I asked the group of seniors to do repairs as it had fallen into shambles. Alex Adams and Julian Stefanovski took the lead and dragged the beaten ship to Julian's driveway a mile from the stadium. I gave the boys money for the repairs and was happy to delegate the task. Later in the year I learned that on the move from the stadium to Julian's driveway the boat literally split in half. The boys chose not to tell me and got some dads involved in reconstructing the frame. Whether they were scared to tell me or took the bull by the horn, I greatly appreciated how these kids ultimately handled the project.

THE BANNERS

In 2013 our consecutive playoff appearance run had stretched to fifteen straight years. Many years earlier, Coach Bob purchased banners we could hang on the stadium north fence line facing inward. The word, PLAYOFF, was printed in orange and outlined in white on black banners. Following the word, PLAYOFF, was every year we had qualified. Even today, the banners create an amazing backdrop for the field and continually remind not only our players but also opposing players of the program's success.

The ability to hang and take down the banners quickly was engineered by our multi-talented statistician, Jim Labuhn. Buhny, as we all called him, put the banners on long skinny PCV pipes with hooks that the kids could carry out of the locker room and lay on the fence line as part of the pregame setup. Groups of Mariners were designated to set up and break down the banners after the games. It was another way to make the stadium, which was a shared stadium, our own on game day.

On Friday, September 6, 2013, the Mariners hosted their first home game, which was also the first league game in the Macomb Athletic Conference Gold Division. The Mariners had transitioned out of a local league, the St. Clair Area League (SCAL) in the 90s, to a northern Detroit mega league. The move allowed us to fill our schedule with opponents who would generate strong playoff point accumulation and fill our schedule with guaranteed crossover games. As the success of the program grew, it became difficult to find non-league opponents who would play us. The Sterling Heights Stallions were first up in the competitive MAC Gold conference. A formula utilized at the time for league alignment put an emphasis on the program's past win/loss success. As a result, the Mariners were forced into a division where the average school enrollment of their opponents was nearly twice the size of Marine City High School.

Home games at East China Stadium were an absolute joy for our community. Tailgaters usually assembled in the southeast corner of the parking complex as early as 4:30 for a 7:00 game. Alcohol consumption was a given for that large a group of tailgaters, but authorities did little to curb it. We quickly learned that the local sheriff had no interest in upsetting potential voters, so he treated the scene with a *see no evil, hear no evil* mentality.

The Friday night air was filled with the deep soothing voice of our beloved stadium announcer, Dave Scheel. Dave was a counselor at Marine City High School and earlier in his career had made radio announcements. He was the most professional stadium announcer in southeast Michigan. There was no gimmicky, "get the keys out for a key play" hype when he announced; he simply let the game do the talking and kept to that script. He was a brilliant advocate for Mariner football and a prominent historian of the program. When he eventually retired in 2018, we thought we could never replace him, but former Mariner, Fred Winzer, stepped in and has done a wonderful job.

The press box also housed our Channel 6 announcers, Craig Zimmerman, and Jerry Basset. They would call the game for an eventual cable replay at midnight. Both men were incredibly supportive of Mariner football with Jerry having done some coaching with Jerry Warkentien in the 70s. The kids and the rest of the community eagerly awaited these midnight versions of the game.

Our marching band, led by one of my all-time favorite co-workers, David Urhig, was 100 members strong and always assembled early in the south end of the complex. Our cheerleaders, who were coached by Mrs. Jen Fregetto, were there early to set up their boxes and the sidelines for the girls' routines. This soupy combination of tailgaters, band members, and cheerleaders created a noise that was both a blessing and a curse. The buzz made it clear to the Mariners that game time was approaching, but it also had the tendency to create great distractions. The result was an anticipatory environment that was absolutely electric.

On this night, the Mariners came out from under the bleacher tunnel and circled the field in their normal pre-game routine. They assembled in long stretch lines and started the unified count chants through all the predetermined stretches. I played in high school for a coach that believed in silence, when stretching as a team. Coach Drath would say, "Listen to *their* noise, and let that sink in to get you ready." Coach Bob believed in the opposite, "Be loud and let them know you're ready for war!" Regardless of how I felt, I was smart enough to not mess with tradition, so we maintained many of the pre-game rituals that Coach Bob had created.

Coming into the Sterling Heights game we looked to improve our offensive efficiency, which had been hit and miss during the Richmond game. After just three plays, the Mariners kicked to the Stallions and immediately forced them to punt, The Mariner offense set up on the 50-yard line where we ran three straight run plays and failed to get a first down. On the ensuing punt from Dana O'Rourke, the Mariners forced a fumble and regained possession, and then...the offense started to click. Big-chunk-plays on the ground from Jarrett Mathison and Tate Sapienza got the Mariners to the 10-yard line. As the defense focused on stopping our run game, Coach Letson called a play action pass and Alex Merchant found Pete Patsalis in the corner of the end zone. The Mariners were on the board first, Olivia Viney added the extra point, and the Mariners were up 7-0. Tate Sapienza was a great complement to Jarrett as Tate offered excellent speed with his wiry frame. Tate was a hard worker in the weight room and difficult to bring down even though he carried only 145 pounds on his lithe body. He also fought his way through some tough times at home and continued to maintain the most positive outlook and frame of mind—a character trait that made him an excellent leader by example.

The Mariner defense again held the Stallion's with three offensive plays and a punt, which was downed on our five-yard line. A converted linebacker, senior, Kyle Scharnweber, who had never played defensive line before, led the defensive line. Our upcoming sophomores, Denny Fitzsimmons and Jacob Headlee, were a great balance to our established linebacker, Eddie Crampton. Our depth at linebacker allowed us to make the move with Kyle, but his unselfishness and willingness to take on the new role made the move a success. TEAM OVER TALENT again rang loudly through the Mariners.

On the very first play from the five-yard line, Alex Merchant hit Pete Patsalis on a tight end seam route right down the middle of the field and Pete was off to the races. A 95-yard touchdown pass, and an Olivia Viney extra point put the Mariners up 14-0, and what emerged was the three-headed attack that would carry the Mariners all season. Jarrett Mathison, Tate Sapienza, and Pete Patsalis all enjoyed 1000-yard-plus accomplishments by the end of the season.

The Stallions attempted a swing pass to the left, flat on its next play, and defensive lineman, Scott Steinmetz, got his paw on the Quarterback's arm...forcing the ball to become a lateral pass. Pete Patsalis recovered the fumble and once again the Mariners were on the attack. Tate Sapienza quickly finished the drive with an 18-yard scamper off the left side of the line with our bread-and-butter WING-T-OFF tackle play. We were experimenting with a new concept of huge line splits being promoted by quirky Texas Tech head coach, Mike Leach. Tate took full advantage of a wall and a lane created by Dana O'Rourke, Paul Carbone, Griffin Lictawa, and Kenton Rivard. Having full reins of the offense starting in 2005, I continually looked for ways to strengthen our Wing-T principals, which proved a good fit for this team. The Mariners led midway through the first quarter 21-0.

On the next offensive possession, the Mariners went shot gun and Alex hit Pete on a post route for a big gainer. Alex then connected with Jake Shermetaro, who made a nice run after the catch. We followed with a fullback trap to Trevor Quandt, who got us to the one-yard line. Jarrett finished the drive, and the Mariners still had a 28-0 lead in the first quarter.

The game ended with a running clock, and a 50-13 scoreboard. Alex finished the game, connecting on six of seven passes for 219 yards, and two touchdown passes. When we realized Pete had amassed 134 yards receiving, we knew we had multiple weapons for offense and an aggressive defense that would make us a tough opponent all year. The Mariners were 2-0 overall and 1-0 in the tough MAC Gold conference— separating themselves from other teams.

LESS IS MORE.

THE BEST PIECE of advice I received from Coach Bob regarding summer workouts was that *kids need to be kids in the summer* and *less is more.* Our team is surrounded by programs that require kids to go to multiple 7-on-7 dates and summer workouts. Coach Bob established a schedule for summer workouts that would run Monday through Thursday from 6:00 to 8:00 p.m. If you were free, we wanted you there; if you had a family vacation, then the family came first; if you had a baseball game...go to it and hit the weights on your off nights.

I think our kids and our community families appreciated us not having an *all-or-nothing mentality* about football. Summer is the offseason for all sports, and as a smaller school, we not only had to share athletes but could not afford to force kids to specialize. There were some good Mariner football players we saw very little during the summer because of their work schedule or because they were a high-level baseball player. We were fine with that and thought the most important thing was that we had the school's best athletes on the field in August when practice started.

When I became head coach, I wanted to give the kids options for when they could work out. I also felt we lacked an approach to develop speed and agility in our athletes. This led to creating a schedule for speed training on Monday and Wednesday mornings, with an option to attend at night if that worked better for a player. We continued with our strength conditioning options on Tuesday and Thursday nights and sprinkled in two 7-on-7 dates and a camp at the end of June.

The moment I first thought there was something special about this 2013 team was when I saw the number of kids coming to sessions on Monday and Wednesday *and* the Tuesday and Thursday dates. It turned into a positive feedback system where our athletes intensified their effort each time they stepped into our small auxiliary gym and the weight room. Early in the workouts, I would comment, "It's too quiet in here, talk to your teammates, challenge them." By the end of the summer, the noise that bellowed out of the aux gym during workouts was something we'd never experienced. I remember reading a post on social media from Grant Sharpe's brother and it went something like this, "Waiting to pick up my brother from a Mariner workout, the noise and energy is off the charts. No wonder these guys have success...much respect."

Another beneficial change in the summer of 2013 was the help we received in the weight room from former Mariner,

Ben Pauli. Ben had transitioned into powerlifting and recently graduated from Central Michigan University. He asked if he could help on our lifting nights and I said, "You can run the whole thing, Brother."

Ben's energy was extremely contagious, and he would get to the weight room usually 45 minutes before the start…to set up unique variances of our usual lifts. His ability to explain the rationale behind each lift was mesmerizing, and the kids absorbed every ounce of the magic he provided. Much of the credit for our dominant strength in 2013 was directly tied to Ben, and it created momentum the offensive line specifically maintained during the season.

Following the home-opener victory over Sterling Heights, we traveled to another MAC Gold opponent and secured a victory over Lake Shore 35-7. The following week was a league cross over victory against Clawson 56-21, which we followed with another league cross over win at East Detroit 27-0. While most people would think the opposite, Coach Bob once stated. "The best time to challenge your team is after a win!"

The East Detroit game and the week of practice that followed is burned into my memory as the turning point of that season. We did not play particularly well against East Detroit. In fact, I was so frustrated with our mediocre play I told Coach Letson after the game he should talk to the team alone because, "I have nothing good to say!" Although we won the game 27-0 and secured a shutout against a very athletic team, the penalties and missed opportunities on offense, and an overall lack of enthusiasm created a *nails on the chalkboard* nagging buzz in my head. The whole bus ride home I debated with myself, *how am I going to address the team in the aux gym?*

I am far from a psychologist, nor am I trained in mental persuasion, but I decided, in a three-minute tirade, to throw the entire blame on the team's lack luster performance on ME!

"I am the worst coach in Michigan because I can't get my team to stop holding during pass plays. Evidently, I can't get the team to stop jumping offsides, or to stop lining up incorrectly on offense. I must be the worst fricking coach in Michigan because our defense won't wrap up when we tackle. The team isn't responding to my attempts to get them to swarm to the ball. I should be fired, there is no reason I should still be the coach on this team."

Like a volcano building pressure, my emotions got the best of me, and I became continually more enraged as I spouted my WORST COACH IN AMERICA rationale. I chose not to make much eye contact but the few times I did, it was clear the kids were as confused as hell about what was going on. I don't remember how I ended the tirade, but I know I stormed out of the aux gym and left them alone to figure out the next step.

On Monday I felt no better about our performance—especially after watching the game film. I decided that a point of emphasis needed to be made right away and I directed the kids to a parking lot drainage ditch that ran between the tennis courts and the old practice field.

THE DITCH DRILLS

Before the Ward Street athletic complex renovation, the Mariners would practice on the southeast corner of the property behind Marine City Middle School. Near the east end zone of the practice field was a drainage ditch that ran parallel to the back of the end zone. Behind that drainage ditch were tall grass plants and a marshy mix of other vegetation. Coach Bob had frequently utilized the ditch in conditioning where he would tell the players to get into the ditch and bear crawl out on the whistle. Our athletes would stand up at the top of the ditch and jog back to the bottom for the next whistle. And the DITCH DRILL was born.

We had not practiced on that field for several years and our 2013 team had no idea where the ditch was—let alone what the ditch drill involved but, on that Monday, I decided this team needed to learn a little Mariner history. At the start of practice, I directed the team to the ditch and gave them no other directions. I drove the Durango around the school and onto the old practice field, parking it in the end zone at the top of the ditch. My mindset became that of a scientist-engaged in observation and recording what I surveyed before me. Some kids smiled as they waited for my instructions, but most knew something was up—especially after my tirade in the aux gym. The captains noticed me piercing the smiling group with deadly stares and immediately ran over to them and told them to shut up.

I explained the ditch drill and blew the whistle for the first bear crawl climb. I had one little twist on the ditch drill—each player had to put another player on his back as he crawled up the ditch.

"This one is for the offensive line holding three times on Friday," I calmly stated.

The whistle blew again, "This one is for the two offside penalties called on our defensive line."

The whistle blew again, "This one is for the three dropped passes that were perfectly thrown," I stated with a dry, emotionless voice.

And so, they endured...for nearly 10 minutes, with both coaches and players looking at me with a *how much more of this do we have to endure* stare. At one point, one of our bigger kids had trouble breathing, and I directed Coach Whymer to pull him out and check on him. I remember having a tennis ball in my hand and tossing it up and down the whole time. This may have added to the notion in some of their minds that I had lost it and was completely off the rails. I knew for us to become a better team, each player needed to know our expectations were not being met unless we improved each week.

As the players jogged over to the practice field, I could hear Paul Carbone complain to the team, "That was bullshit; I had f***g Bruce to carry!" The exercise was no joy for Bruce Penrod either as both boys were well over 250 pounds.

Our next league opponent, the Lakeview Huskies, were scheduled to play us on the following Friday despite having twice our enrollment. The Mariners were locked in and ready for the match up and it became obvious as we ran the opening kickoff back to our dedicated return called the Starburst. On this night, the four deep backs were Jarrett Mathison, Tate Sapienza, Pete Patsalis, and Trevor Quandt who formed a diamond starting at the 20-yard line. The ball was squib kicked right down the middle and handled well by Jarrett. He was the point of the diamond and asked to handle any ball he could get to. We looked to put an outstanding baseball player in this position because we had more success in the return. The answer from most teams was to squib kick the football on the ground. Jarrett. an excellent short stop, absorbed the kick directly into his belly area, Pete Patsalis immediately converged and took the hand-off, with Tate and Trevor sequenced through Jarrett and took their fakes in the opposite direction. Four backs exploding away from the central point of the ball, created the illusion of the starburst. Pete took the ball down the Mariner sideline racing nearly 80 yards for the opening score.

WHERE DID THE STARBURST ORIGINATE?

In 1988, my second year at Marine City, my brother, Jim Glodich, shared with me a kickoff return that his school was running down in San Antonio Texas. Jim had moved down there in 1982 when teaching jobs in Michigan grew scarce. He coached in the middle school but learned that football in Texas was highly advanced and middle school teams were running some high-level stuff. He sent a video tape explaining the blocking schemes for each return and the running back sequence.

I shared this return play with Coach Bob, and he was enthusiastic about a multi-fake return since it went hand in hand with his overall WING-T concept and misdirection philosophy. I have spoken several times at clinics, sharing this information with fellow coaches, and it drives me crazy when I hear a school say they were the first to run the STARBURST in Michigan. They are full of crap—it started in Marine City in 1988!

On our next offensive possession, we applied strategies that were a good fit with quarterback, Alex Merchant's skill set. Marine City had traditionally used offensive run-based formations that incorporated two tight ends. With Alex we used formations that could *spread* the defense such as three receivers to one side, no back sets, and shot gun with two backs—to mention a few. The drive was a perfect blend of run and pass, which utilized multi formations and was capped off with a 35-yard touchdown pass from Alex to Pete on a fade route. Our coaching staff quickly realized that the offense was taking on a whole new and improved persona, and it was exciting to watch.

The Mariners finished the night with a 55-6 victory over Lakeview but most important, we improved in all phases of the game. Following the customary handshake lines, the Mariners headed to the southeast corner of the end zone for another stadium tradition. The Mariners would stand roughly six feet apart in the end zone and face the boat, then the cannon would fire, and all the Mariners would fall straight back onto the turf as if they had been shot by the cannon. I believe that tradition started with our 2011 team who went undefeated and made it to Ford Field—only to lose to Zeeland West High School. That team was loaded with hard-working, tough-nosed kids. Aaron Loconsole was a dominant linebacker, Anthony Scarcelli was one of the best running backs ever to come out of Marine City, and the Kroll twins with Adam at quarterback and Alex at defensive line were tenacious competitors.

To this day, I genuinely believe the regional final win over Detroit Crockett in 2011 was the greatest underdog win in our program's history.
Multiple Division 1 athletes packed that team, as well as a defensive back still playing in the NFL, but the Mariners ground out a 15-7 historic win.

The team's focus was reestablished and next up for the Mariners was longtime rival—the Marysville Vikings. The Mariners would travel to Walt Braun stadium (named after their legendary coach who held the reins for 30-plus years). It was a stadium where we had little success in the early years of Coach Bob's tenure, but the tide had turned in the late 90s and we were finally enjoying a nice run of our own after years of failure.

6

THE PICTURE, THE HEIST, THE MAP.

"**SUMMER 1989. AT** 15 years old, they were at the midpoint of our adolescence. They were somewhere in between boys and men, though fully cocksure of their place in life. Like most young men at that age, they knew it all and knew no fear."

~ #47 Mike Simek Class of '92

One goal in authoring this book is to share major historical events I believe helped to shape the Mariner football program. As Walt Braun and the Marysville Viking dominance ran rampant over Marine City in the late 80s and early 90s, the following is such an important event sit was, in my opinion, a major turning point in the mindset of our athletes.

In the summer of 1989, Mike Simek and Chris Gabler, two eager Mariners coming up through the ranks of the program, hatched a plan. I was lucky enough to coach them on the JV team in 1989 but also in '90 and '91 when I transitioned to offensive coordinator on varsity. Like sponges, they soaked up every word that Coach Bob spit out and at that point in his career, Coach Bob was modeling and replicating a full-blown Woody Hayes impersonation.

As Mike Simek remembered, "Coach unabashedly stole a page from the greatest rivalry in the history of sports (Michigan–Ohio State) and removed *Marysville* and *Vikings* from the vernacular of every Mariner...an edict that perhaps even cascaded to the teaching of the Scandinavian incursions during history classes. Like the silly *Suckeyes* who cross out the *M's* across campus in Columbus the week of the Michigan game, the Marine City football team wasn't allowed to even think about those horribly offensive pejoratives, let alone speak them out loud."

Their plan was simple. Steal a picture of the enemy leader (Walt Braun) in the Marysville McDonald's®, and later burn the picture in the homecoming bonfire before the Marysville game. The two recruited a third member into their larceny gang...the 9½ fingered bandit, Jake Achatz. (*For reference Chris Gabler wore #51, Mike Simek wore #47, and Jake Achatz wore #41.*)

Under the facade of a bowling excursion to the Marysville Viking lanes, the gang convinced Chris Gabler's mom to drive them unsupervised into enemy territory. They did in fact, go bowling. The boys even secured the score sheet as proof but make no mistake—the trio was on a mission, and as focused and determined as John Belushi in *Animal House.*

Mike described the event, noting, "The section was empty. No one was there to witness the heist. Still, we had to execute with absolute precision and a high sense of urgency. Number 51 struck with the speed and brutality akin to Dick Butkus knocking down an opposing running back. With one violent jerk, the picture was removed from the wall and handed off to #41 who quickly stashed it in a nondescript paper bag. It was with a quality of grace and discretion uncharacteristic of awkward adolescent boys that we left the establishment without issue. The extraction mission was a complete success! Glory awaited us."

Amazingly, no one on our staff heard of the heist. For all parties involved it became a distant memory until Week 5 of the season rolled around. Then like a wildfire in the arid west, with homecoming and the Vikings in vision, the heat exploded. Both the Mariners and the Vikings came into that match up with an unlikely 2-2 record, but a league championship and supreme bragging rights were still in the balance. The crafty Walt Braun had known of the picture heist but sat on the information all summer long. When Week 5 rolled around, he used that heist to his advantage. He called our Athletic Director, Jerry Warkentien, and relayed the information he had gathered. "Mr. Warkentien, I have from a good source that a picture was stolen from the Marysville McDonald's, and it was taken by one of your football players. I want the picture returned before the end of the week, and in turn I will not share my information with the police."

There is no doubt in my mind Walt shared the heist with his players and used it to heighten motivation for another Mariner ass-kicking. That is good coaching! We always look for motivational angles. The knowledge of the players involved being revealed to Coach Bob was clarified when #47 was aggressively questioned during a Wednesday JV pre-game.

"Who has Walt Braun's picture?" Coach Bob barked.

What wasn't evident then, but is now, is that some of the Mariner brethren failed to heed the old Navy adage that "loose lips sink ships." The administration from *the team up north* had learned of their brilliant but treacherous act and requested an unconditional surrender and return of the hard-earned trophy. After beating the varsity into submission by interrogation through countless down-ups, #47's older brother divulged that his younger brother *might* know who had the picture. That led to the forced march down to the JV team to interrogate #47, who met Coach Staskiewicz' hard stare and replied, 'I do, Coach.'"

Simek was quick to recall, "With fire in his eyes, and expletives falling from his mouth, he slapped his clipboard across #47's helmet. Though embarrassing at the time, #47 now remembers it was like being knighted by a king. Number 51 appeared at # 47's shoulders to assume responsibility for his role in the operation before Coach Staskiewicz could take his next breath."

Coach Bob told the players to meet him in the office after practice—a classic teacher/coach move when you're not sure how to discipline a student/athlete. It allows panic to set in on the accused while they wait in utter fear of the upcoming sentencing. The boys asked me at the end of practice, "Are we allowed to play in tomorrow's game, Coach?"

"That's up to the big guy," was my quick and honest response. Their faces went blank, and their jaws dropped. It was at this point the *larceny gang* wondered if it was worth the risk they had taken. If there was one truth in this whole scenario, it was that Mike Simek and Chris Gabler were true competitors and damn good football players. If they were shut out of the Marysville game, it would prove to be the equivalent of a brutal sentencing for a minor crime.

"Once in the coach's office, with the blinds pulled low so no other players could see, it was clear to #47 and #51 that what had just happened at the 50-yard line was perhaps the greatest acting in the history of Marine City High School dramatic performances. Coach Staskiewicz sat behind his desk with the quintessential Cheshire cat's grin. The same was true of the other coaches. Though they professionally disapproved of the player's behavior, the great heist had indeed elevated the trio in the eyes of their beloved coaches. The coaches freakin' loved it!" Mike Simek joyfully recalled.

The joy was fleeting; Coach Bob demanded that the players return the picture directly to Coach Braun at his home. "To make this right, you knuckleheads will return the picture and the frame to Coach Braun tonight. Only if you do this can you play in tomorrow's JV game," was Coach Bob's ultimatum.

That very evening, following Coach Staskiewicz' direction to return the picture to Coach Braun, the players were forced to confide in #51's mother and beg for another ride north, behind enemy lines, to atone for their sins by hand-delivering the picture to Coach Braun—at his house.

With apprehension, they approached his home, knocked on the door, and introduced themselves. With sincere remorse and embarrassment, they asked for forgiveness and returned the picture to him. Considering how disrespectful the athletes' actions were to Coach Braun, they assumed he was going to lay into them and let them know how despicable their behavior was. The opposite proved true! Coach Braun proved to be a true gentleman. In fact, he even chuckled about the escapade, and said, "I am proud you had the fortitude to personally return the picture to me." He also conveyed his respect that they had the stupid courage to do something so juvenile; he knew well how important that rivalry was to Marine City.

"What a great man! In those few precious moments our own *larceny gang* shared with Coach Braun, it was clear why he was so loved by his players. Like coaches Staskiewicz, Scarcelli, and Glodich, Coach Braun was the kind of guy you would love to follow into battle," Mike Simek recollects.

Mike Simek, Chris Gabler, and Jake Achatz never beat Marysville in their time with Mariner football, but they did introduce a change in players' mentality. Marysville had dominated the Mariners for several years and it developed a mindset that the team to the north was unstoppable. As dads who lost to Marysville now watched their sons compete, the message at home was repeated, "As long as Walt's the head coach we won't beat Marysville." But the tenacity of those three men diverted that mental state and converted the mindset into a call for change. It was as if they were screaming, "We will not take this anymore, we will try something new to turn the tide, this cannot continue!" Coach Bob and the Mariners broke through the wall in 1996 and our record flipped the proverbial page of dominance.

In their senior year ('91), when Marine City qualified for the state playoffs, the boys were part of one of the biggest wins in program history. On a bitter cold night on November 8, 1991, the Mariners took on the number one ranked team in the state in the first round of the playoffs. The Oxford Wildcats, coached by the legendary Bud Rowley, were loaded with Division 1 talent and undefeated in Class BB division. With their 9-0 record the team was averaging 31 points a game on offense, while only yielding eight points a game defensively. No one in Michigan gave the Mariners a chance; Oxford was the favorite to return to the state finals after losing in 1990.

> The Mariners Front-7 was a dominant force by year's end and featured defensive ends, Mike Simek and Ben Kaufman.

> The defensive line was led by Andy Scheel, Ryan Pettinger, and Jeff Krause, who protected linebackers Chris Gabler and Brandon Osterland.

On the back end, the sure handed tackling of athletic Matt Closs and Brian Recor anchored a unit of ball-hawking defensive backs.

Hard-hitting corners, Ryan Dunn and Shawn Collins, provided an edge rarely challenged or tested.

On that frigid night, this motivated group of athletes held the Oxford scoring machine to just 25 points but more important, made Oxford work extremely hard for every point scored. Many of the Oxford players were playing on both sides of the ball and by the game's end, fatigue was a factor.

The story of the night was the quick scoring attack of the Mariner WING-T-OFFENSE led by the lightning fast and shifty undersized fullback, Dennis Hall. A massive upset was aided by the Mariner's black forearm pads and the dark November sky.

The Mariner offensive line created holes in the Oxford defense from start to finish—anchored by tight ends, Brian Recor and Brian Beaudua; tackles, Mike Simek and Matt Burmann; guards, Chris Gabler and Mike Piper; and center, Steve Walker.

In the backfield, quarterback, Bobby Donaldson, halfback, Andy Cottrell, and fullback, Dennis Hall, carried out fakes that neutralized the Wildcat talent.

Big play receivers in Mike Wojcik and Adam Sebastian and kicker, Don Seibert, provided scoring threats from everywhere on the field.

The game was a contrast of styles. Oxford would consume large chunks of time with their scoring drives while the Mariners hit several long fullback traps as Dennis Hall racked up insane rushing yards against a top ranked defense. With the final score reading Marine City 48—Oxford 25, the Mariners pulled off an upset no one saw coming. Newspapers across the state would later request comments from Coach Bob and it was the buzz of the night in the coaching world.

Upsets in high school football are not as common as they are in other levels of football, but this was a classic upset and one of mountainous size.

The game would inaugurate and mold the vision that a couple of 15-year-old bandits invented while washing dishes in the back of the Salt Docks restaurant. Mariner football had a vision of achieving greatness through teamwork, hard work, and dedication, creating an unforgettable experience that would last a lifetime.

The game put Marine City on a map of towns known for football. It also put the Mariners on a map of recognition in the state of teams no one can overlook.

It's rewarding to hear outsiders now say, "Marine City, I hear they have a good football program."

7

RIVALRY NUMBER ONE.

THE BUSES WERE loaded, and the Marine City coaching staff huddled behind them were flat out stunned because it had happened again. It wasn't expected; we all believed THIS would be THE YEAR. A Marysville student, walking along the northeast corner of Marysville High School with his girlfriend on his arm asked, "What was the score?"

I answered and took the bait, never thinking it was a set up, "30-8," was my short response.

"Well, maybe next year," the little smart ass replied with a smirk on his face, which epitomized the arrogance that some Marysville fans garnered. It was 1994, and the Mariners had just lost their ninth straight game to the area's premier program, the Marysville Vikings.

In 1985, with Jerry Warkentien at the helm of the program, the Mariners defeated Marysville at the old high school field on Ward Street, in an exciting 4:00 p.m. Friday afternoon game win of 20-7. The Mariners were loaded with talent that year...advancing to the state semifinals and losing to Divine Child (14-0), who eventually won the state Class B championship. In the 1985 Marysville game, the offense was led by a tough-nosed running back named Randy Jones, who dominated the game even though he was dealing with a knee injury going into the game. Eric Gunderson, a true dual threat quarterback, ran a veer offense. Inside linebackers, Tim McConnell and Ron Wesley, led the defense. The Mariners at the time ran a 4-4 defense and were successful because of superior defensive end play led by Ron Rhoades and Kevin Dubay.

Outside linebackers, Bill Enders and Dale Volker, cleaned up anything Rhoades and Dubay would spill out. The secondary featured Darren Brooks, Eric Gunderson, and Mark Niemic, who were all very athletic and could prevent the big play. It always helps to have a defensive lineman who gives big offensive lineman problems; that role was filled to perfection by Alan Ausmus who was a quick, little wrestler. Following the 1985 Mariner win, the Vikings went on a pivotal win streak stretching over 11 years—a streak that eventually led to the formation and success of today's Mariner football program.

Coach Bob would not drive through Marysville, nor would he say their name aloud—only calling Marysville, "THEM." He would put the score of the previous game on a sheet of white typing paper and tape it to the inside of his locker so every day in the coaching office he would be reminded of the simple question that took years to answer, "What do we have to do to beat Marysville?"

They were one of the more dominant programs in the state, not just in our area. They claimed state championships in 1986 and again in 1992 and their coach was legendary. Walt Braun created a formula we mimicked, which was the biggest compliment we could give him. Marysville had a full platoon team that played 11 guys on offense and 11 different guys on defense. They ran an offense, also based on Wing-T concepts, and involved discipline fakes. They had a coaching staff that stayed together for many years and benefited from the outstanding defensive coordinator, Jim Venia.

In 1996 the Mariners would lose in the regular season to THEM, 35-13, but would turn around just three weeks later and face them in the opening round of the state playoffs. That year's Mariner team was loaded with tough-nosed kids who exhibited an incredible competitive spirit. It didn't matter whether it was football or checkers, many on the team would compete with an intensity rarely found in today's high school athlete. We were blessed to have Kyle Zimmerman at quarterback; twins, Brent and Bryan Osterland, in the backfield, and speedy Jeff Bradley as our go-to receiver. John Ikera, Ralph Onesko, Nathan Smith, and Vinny Collins anchored the offensive line. Steve Pauli, Joe Krantz, Jarod Carpenter, and Pat Phelan were the strength of our defense. On that day, we hosted the playoff game at East China stadium, and it was a complete mud bowl. Conditions on the field were about as bad as they could be.

Marysville was led by a huge fullback that year and we had our hands more than full trying to stop him. Our defensive line made piles and prevented him from getting any head of steam. The Mariners scored just 12 points that day—six coming from a defensive scoop and score. Joe Krantz penetrated the offensive line and hit the Viking running back in the back field; Jarod Carpenter scooped up the fumble and had a short run into the end zone. The final score was 12-7 Marine City, with the Mariners breaking a 11-year victory drought.

This victory was one of the monumental wins in the program's history as it now gave confidence to future teams that the Vikings were beatable.

We knew if we were going to be competitive year in and year out with Marysville, we had to follow the Vikings' lead-in program development. Starting in 1998 we went full platoon as well, and this dramatically changed the way we practiced. By dedicating our players to either offense or defense we could put our best athletes on special teams. We structured practice where individual skill development could be inserted more often, and team sessions allowed the team to expand both offensive and defensive concepts. Backup players received more attention and more snaps in live sessions—a game plan that also allowed us to pit best-against-best a few times during the week.

Finally, we knew by platooning, our overall fatigue in a game would be reduced, and players would have fresh legs in the fourth quarter. It paid off immediately in 1998 with the

Mariners winning the ultimate rivalry game 13-0. Over the next 18 meets leading to the 2013 game, the Mariners had turned the tide and were victorious in 16 out of the 18 matchups—including 10 straight wins of our own going into the 2013 grid iron battle.

The 2013 game featured the 4-2 Vikings—powered by a big and physical offensive line and a talented quarterback. Marysville took the opening kickoff and marched down the field with a 16-play drive that consumed seven minutes on the clock. The Vikes failed on the two-point conversion. It was 6-0 Vikings with five minutes remaining in the first quarter. The Mariners struggled on their first two possessions failing to achieve a first down. The Vikings made it to the Mariner 28-yard line and were poised to score again. Big defensive plays from Scott Steinmetz, Dennis Fitzsimmons, Alec Adams, and Kyle Scharnweber forced the Vikes into a fourth-down scenario. On fourth-down the Vikings attempted a slip screen into the right flats, and had it set up well. Jarett Mathison caught the ball after it bounced off the receiver and ran 73 yards for a pick 6. The scoreboard read 7-6 Mariners with 8:05 remaining in the second quarter.

Another Marysville punt was forced by the Mariner defense, and Pete Patsalis returned it for 35 yards. On the first play from scrimmage, a speedy Tate Sapienza took a sweep play off right tackle, 50 yards well into the Viking red zone. Four plays later, on a short yardage wedge play, Jarrett scored his second TD of the game, and the Mariners were up 14-6 with four minutes left in the second quarter.

On Marysville's next possession, the quarterback was brutally sandwiched between Alec Adams and Kevin Fitzsimmons in their backfield and the ball popped free. Alec scooped the ball off the turf and scrambled into the end zone. The scoreboard read 21-6 Mariners with 3:49 left in the half.

Marysville mounted another strong drive and scored on their next possession on a swing pass from 35 yards out, but again failed on the two-point conversion; 21-12 Mariners with 3:10 left at half.

The Mariners answered the call with just one play—Alex Merchant found a wide-open Pete Patsalis on a tight end seam route. Pete rambled 67 yards, finally being brought down at the one-yard line. Pete would hear the dreaded words from me on Monday in our film session.

"Good backs and receivers never get tackled at the one-yard line."

Jarett finished the two-play drive, and the Mariners were up 28-12 with 2:46 left.

On Marysville's next possession our rival again mounted a nice drive but fumbled around the 50-yard line with just 30 seconds remaining in the half. Coach Letson put the Mariners in a 2x2 spread formation and we ran four vertical routes, with Alex hitting Jarett in perfect stride on the left hash, where he ran untouched into the end zone. The play was called back with a holding call—negating the score. With only 10 seconds left in the half, we made our last play call.

The Mariners have long been known statewide for our effective FULLBACK TRAP. We call this play on any down, at any location on the field. Sticking with what we did best, we put Jarrett back to fullback and ran Twins 2x2 against the Marysville defense. Ethan Cleve and Josh Albo created the perfect double team on the nose guard, as Paul Carbone from his tackle position scooped inside for a vicious linebacker block. Kenton Rivard with his 6-2, 280-pound frame trapped their down lineman and Jarett was off to the races. It was the carefully articulated downfield blocks implemented by Adam Walendowski, Jake Shermatero, and Griffen Lictawa that allowed Jarett to weave 50 plus yards and break away from the defenders to score—JUST AS THE CLOCK RAN OUT.

The half ended with the Mariners up 35-12 and we were scheduled to receive the second half kickoff. On the opening drive of the second half, Alex Merchant found a wide-open Dana O'Rourke on another seam route and Tate Sapienza finished the drive with a sweep play off right tackle. The score now stood at 41-12 with just under 10 minutes left in the third quarter. What transpired next was an amazing swing in momentum in a truly short time. The game went from 14 to 6 to 41-12 in just six minutes of game time, showcasing an opportune defense and an explosive offense. Confidence ran high in the Mariners as they looked forward to their inter-district rival, the St. Clair Saints, in a game that would decide the MAC Gold league championship.

THE FIRE.

HER TEMPER WAS legendary on Virginia Street in Warren, Michigan. The houses were 20 feet apart, just wide enough for a driveway to run to the back of the yard. If I were in trouble, our neighbors could hear it, their neighbors could hear it, and my buddy, Gary Olsen, who lived across the street and two doors down could hear it. "You G** D**n son of a b***es," was her go-to line.

Were we playing basketball in the back yard and the ball hit the back of the house, within 10 seconds we would hear her angry response out the back window. We knew it was coming and would laugh, which only fueled her anger. "If that ball hits the house again, I am going to beat your ass," was also a common response. By that time, I was a head taller than my 5-2 full-blooded Italian mother with her crowning glory of jet-black hair.

When we were younger, during the summer we would go to Westview Elementary for Warren's Parks and Recreation Program. One year we made key chains out of skinny plastic rope, which we would weave into a small, square structure. Being the overachiever, I made one well over a foot long, when most kids had stopped at three inches. I brought it home and showed it to my mom and she liked it and asked to keep it. I happily turned it over to her, feeling proud that I made something she liked. Two days later I watched her try to whip my older brother John's backside with that same foot long key chain! Rarely did she ever accomplish her goal of physically disciplining her kids. Our speed was no match for her. Our ability to dive under the beds allowed us to escape many angry tirades and when my dad would come home, we would explain, "Dad, she just goes crazy," and he would understand and tell us to lay low for a while. The key chain's life was short-lived! Mom hung it in the pantry for quick access should we make her angry; it disappeared one day, but no one ever took credit for its disappearance. Losing the key chain mattered little to Mom...she had other options and utilized them in future futile mother/son chases.

The greatest anger I ever saw my mother display was one summer night when my brother, John, and I were downstairs playing ping-pong. My older brother, Jim, somehow enraged my mom. To this day we remain clueless about what he did to ignite her. He stormed down the basement stairs and went into the back storage area where he locked himself in a half bathroom at the end of the hall. Two minutes later we heard heavy feet stomping down the stairs. Mom had stopped halfway down the stairs where the wall was cut out for a window, and with a frying pan in her hand she used language I had never heard from her before, "Where is that mother f***er?" My brother John and I literally dove under the ping-pong table and huddled together in fear.

I am a biology major and understand genetics and have no doubt that my competitive fire comes from my mom. I was always fascinated that she could go from the stereotypical Italian housewife cooking incredible lasagna, to a full-blown rage—in a matter of seconds. For better or worse this trait seemed to have been passed down to me, especially in coaching. Her constant message rang through all chores or tasks she asked us to complete, "Do things the right way, and finish the job." When my dad would work on house projects, my mom was famous for setting up a supervisor's chair in the vicinity and relaying feedback to him all during the project.

Polar opposites, my parents! I was always amazed at the contrast in temperaments of my mom and dad. My dad never spanked me, but I still feared the possibilities. Both my parents were outstanding athletes. There were no organized sports for women at Denby High School in Detroit in the 1940s, but my uncle Bob (D'Alessandro) would share stories of how Mom would hold her own playing baseball and other sports with the neighborhood boys. She would be the only girl allowed to play with them because she was that good. My dad was a national champion gymnast who competed with the Catholic Sokol Gymnastic organization.

This drive to *do things the right way* emanated from my mom's dad, Luigi D'Alessandro. Throughout most of my childhood, Grandpa would come over every Sunday for dinner, which was always the same dish—lasagna. During the summer months he would walk the yard with me and point out weeds that needed to be pulled in the flower beds. As I got into my teens, I loved to ask him questions about his immigration to the States. At age 15, he came over alone and falsified his papers as the legal travel age was 16. Somewhere outside Rome, in the Province of L'Aquila, lies the small town of Navelli, which he left. He talked about arriving with only a few dollars in his pocket and one suitcase. Connecting with family already established in Canada and the States, he worked several labor jobs before settling in Detroit. It was clear he was a perfectionist and passed this on to my mother, who passed it on to her third son.

Mom was my biggest supporter and missed none of my games. She was exceptionally vocal at games, to where it embarrassed me at times—especially in baseball, which was her favorite sport. We came to an understanding that if she came to my high school games, she needed to tone it down. On the flip side, she was never afraid to give me tough feedback after a game. I laugh when I see parents today use the "it doesn't matter if you win or lose, as long as you have fun mentality" with their kids. My mom was a competitor and if we didn't win, she would tell me what needed to change. This might have been my mom's greatest insight...the notion of what needed to change and ideas of how to make it happen. She was modeling great coaching, and I didn't even know it.

When I started my coaching career at Marine City, my parents' dedication to supporting me never wavered. Whether my team was playing JV football, JV baseball, or varsity volleyball...they were committed to seeing as many games as possible and the other parents in Marine City welcomed them with open arms. My mom was remarkably friendly and quickly conversed with anyone who approached her. My dad was socially awkward at times and as a result my mom did most of the talking for him. If I ever tried to explain to co-workers or to other Marine City parents about my mom's temper, they refused to believe me saying, "Your mom is the sweetest thing." As Mom aged her temper faded and I loved her coming to my kids' tee ball, or biddy basketball games. I could see the joy in her face as she watched them compete.

I was raised by great parents who believed in discipline and hard work and never took things for granted. Every time I visit the cemetery, I consider the character foundation they laid for us; it is one of which I am now extremely proud, and I make a point to say, "Thank you."

THE RIVALRY TO END ALL RIVALRIES.

"JOSH PRIEBE AND BOB SHARNWEBER are the only two people from St. Clair that we don't hate," was a common thread we impressed upon our kids during this rivalry week. Josh was an outstanding player for us who transferred from St. Clair in the early 90s because we offered wrestling, and they did not. He became a team captain and was one of the best offensive linemen we ever produced. His work ethic was unmatched, and he would spend time every day after practice working on whatever skills he thought needed improvement.

To this day, the vision of one man all alone working on the blocking sled, in the steel chutes, or on the agile bags remains seared into my memory.

Josh went on to compete in wrestling and graduate from the Naval Academy in Annapolis, Maryland, and is now a police officer. His dad, Dr. Mike Priebe, was our team doctor for years and would be on our sideline most Friday nights. Doc Priebe was an incredible asset and would get players into his office on Saturday morning for quick evaluations or treatment.

Bob Sharnweber, or "Sharny" as we loved to call him, was our team trainer for years and hosted the coaches' party after every St. Clair game. He was under-appreciated as the trainer for St. Clair and Coach Bob Staskiewicz convinced Sharny to jump ship and come over to the *dark side*...where he instantly improved our program.

Sharny had a great feel for high school athletics and was spot-on with injury diagnosis during his time spent with us. Being active in the St. Clair community, he could provide us with nuggets of information and gossip swirling around the town during rivalry week. The combination of Sharny and Doc Priebe was so valuable we told other coaches that through this combined expertise, our team was able to have one or two more wins a year.

The dislike of St. Clair was nothing our coaching staff produced, although we played on the energy. It was a deep-rooted dislike between the towns, which created strong voter turnouts whenever the school administration attempted to create one big common high school with bond proposals. Marine City was characterized as a blue-collar town, with residents working locally at some of the plastic plants or commuting down towards Detroit to one of the car companies. Because of my blue-collar upbringing in Warren, Michigan, I felt connected with the town and the people.

St. Clair, on the other hand, was known as the white-collar professional town and in the eyes of many Marine City residents, an air of arrogance permeated both the town and the school. Whether it was perceived or real, our kids felt they were constantly disrespected, which created an incredible energy during rivalry week.

As Coach Bob's vision for the program took shape, the Marine City football team claimed dominance in the Mariner/Saints rivalry. Leading up to the 2013 game, the Mariners had won 27 out of the prior 29 games. Coach Bob continued momentum in the series with five straight wins before experiencing a loss. Then following his one defeat, Bob racked up 12 more years of victories before he retired. Coach Bob's record against St. Clair was 17-1. And, although Coach Scarcelli lost his first contest with the Saints in 2005, he went on to six straight wins before retiring in 2011.

In my first game as head coach in the ongoing rivalry (2012), the Mariners came in as a huge underdog to a talented St. Clair team. It was a strong, undefeated contender that was 7-0 and averaging 45 points a game offensively, while only giving up four points a game defensively. The MAC Gold championship was up for grabs in Week 8 game of the season. Thanks to the efforts of defensive coordinator Matt Pollack and players Jake Pelshaw, AJ Rodriguez, DJ Burns, and Sam Honaker, the Mariners achieved an upset win. The win gave the Mariners the MAC Gold championship and possession of the rivalry Bell Trophy, which the Mariners paraded around the field in the post-game celebration.

This particular game was one of the most satisfying wins in my entire coaching career and our enthusiastic post-game celebration created even more friction as we moved into the 2013 game. If memory serves me, a couple of our coaches may have posed midfield during the post-game pandemonium with their best WWF Hulk Hogan imitations.

10

LESSONS LEARNED.

IT WAS A challenge to eat anything the day we played the Saints. My nerves seem to have gotten the best of me...even though I have been coaching for 20-plus years. I remember saying to friends, "You would think that I would have developed some coping mechanisms to deal with nerves after all these years, but that isn't true." I headed to the stadium that day at my usual time of 4:30 p.m. Dad was with me, as he loved to go early and chat in the press box with Dave Sheel, our stadium announcer.

As I entered the parking lot, it was immediately apparent the crowd would be massive. Tail gaiting was going on in two areas. The Mariner crowd loved the southeast corner of the lot, which hugged that particular corner of the field. The Saints crowd gathered at the northwest corner of the lot that hugged the performing arts building. Even in tail gaiting there was a North/South divide that defined this rivalry.

Several blankets were taped down in the bleachers to mark territory for loyal fans. Some of the Mariners were on the field engaged in their pre-game rituals, but what made this game so different was that the Saints were there just as early and just as engaged. At most home games our kids had the field to themselves in this early phase, but not on this night.

When we came out for warmups at 6:00 p.m., the crowd in the stands was already established and there was an enthusiastic roar as we circled the field. It was a beautiful night for football, and two 7-0 teams were about to do battle for the MAC Gold championship. There was no need for a pre-game hype speech; our players were emotionally locked in and ready for a four-quarter war. I remember looking across the field and seeing several Saints flags attached to the top row of the visiting bleachers, and several banners hanging on the lowest fence line. The Saints were all in on this night and their fan base was out in mass.

The Mariners took the opening kickoff but had no success with the Starburst kickoff return. On our first play from scrimmage, we ran a fullback trap to Jarett Mathison where one of the Saints' defenders slanted low and hard toward our center and his helmet hit Jarett's knee straight on. Jarett got up from the hit and was limping badly, but he wanted to stay in the game. He tried to line up for the next play but continued to struggle, so we used a timeout to get reorganized.

We failed to move the ball down the field and ended up punting near midfield. On the Saints' opening drive their quarterback, Jared Tobey, took an option fake and ran down their sideline for a long run. Pete Patsalis ran him down and tackled him at the four-yard line. The officials somehow misinterpreted the lines on our field and signaled it as a touchdown. They refused to talk with me about their mistake and placed the ball at the three-yard line for the extra point. The St. Clair staff called a run play not realizing that it was an extra point attempt, and we stuffed it! Repeated attempts on my part to get an explanation failed and the officials placed the ball on the 40-yard line for the kickoff. The scoreboard read a disconcerting 6-0.

On our next drive, Jarett returned to the game as his pain had subsided. We moved the ball across midfield and into their territory but failed on a fourth-down conversion. The St. Clair team quickly capitalized on the play and scored on a 30-yard run and converted the two-point conversion to make the score 14-0. Once again, the Mariners found it challenging to advance the ball and ended up turning it over to the Saints. The Saints capitalized on the situation by scoring on a long drive that took up a lot of time on the clock. With 4:41 left in the second quarter, the scoreboard displayed 22-0. The Saints' fans were in pandemonium since the large lead and the Mariners shut out was something rarely experienced. In the joy of celebrating touchdowns and significant plays, the Saints used a portable foghorn to make noise, and while the Mariner cannon was silent, the horn filled the night air with its sound.

With a 22-point deficit, we transitioned out of our initial game plan and opened the offense to take advantage of Alex Merchant's passing abilities. Alex connected with Pete Patsalis on a seam route; Pete dodged a few Saints and took the pass to the end zone. The extra point attempt failed with a bad snap and the board read 22-6 going into halftime.

At halftime we reminded the team of the comeback with Richmond in Game 1, and of a similar success story the prior year during the St. Clair game. We made our adjustments and felt the kids were locked in and ready for the second half. Jarett seemed to manage the pain in his knee and our passing game appeared to give our offense some new life.

St. Clair took the second half kickoff and in just three plays scored. They converted the extra point, and the scoreboard read 29-6 with 11:01 remaining in the third quarter. It became obvious that St. Clair was an outstanding football team. Their head coach, Bill Nesbitt, was a former assistant on our staff, and I still consider him one of the best teachers/coaches with whom I have ever worked. He had a talented group of athletes which included a couple of running backs with great speed and offensive and defensive lines that championed both size and strength. His defense was physical and swarmed to the ball. They would go on to reach the Division 3 semifinals in 2013 and were an extra point away from reaching Ford Field.

They were the real deal in 2013 and we were learning this firsthand.

We hit pay dirt on our next drive with a 60-yard flare pass to Jarett, followed by a fullback trap to Trevor Quandt to reach the end zone. We failed on a two-point conversion making the score 29-12 with 9:55 left in the third quarter. The Saints answered the challenge in just three plays and now were up 37-12. We returned the favor in just two plays with a 55-yard run from Jarett Mathison to make the score 37-19 with 8:34 remaining in the third quarter. The stadium was in complete hysteria with the back-and-forth flow of the game. The constant buzz in the air made it virtually impossible to communicate with our players on the field. That we were screaming at the top of our lungs was not an overstatement.

Our defense made adjustments, and we forced the Saints into a three-and-out. On our second play of the drive, we ran a screen play to Jarrett. Offensive linemen, Griffen Lictawa, Kenton Rivard, and Josh Albo created the perfect alley for our man to race 50 yards for the score. Alex did a great job of drawing the defense up field and floated the perfect pass to Jarett. Things were getting interesting and flashbacks of the 2012 comeback rose from the bleachers as we watched the Mariner fans gain strength. The scoreboard read 37-26 with 6:20 left in the third.

After that, the Saints made a drive that placed them on our 10-yard line and in a position to score again. The defensive line plays of Scott Steinmetz and Kenton Rivard created havoc and forced a fumble that linebacker, Eddie Crampton, dove on and recovered in midair. With 2:20 left in the third quarter, the Mariners gained possession on our 10-yard line, trailing by only 11 points.

In just two plays, a toss to Tate Sapienza and a pass to Pete Patsalis, the team put the Mariners at midfield and driving. On first down, we ran a fullback trap to Jarett who scampered to our sideline, fighting off several Saints' defenders. As he neared our sideline and went down, our guard, Ethan Cleve, blocked one of the Saints so forcefully he flew into our sideline. We were called for a late hit, which added to the official's incompetence on that night. Our sideline went nuts reacting to the refs' call and to that of our loyal and dedicated librarian and yearbook editor, Kathy Reichle, who was struck by the flying St. Clair player. She had wandered a little too close to the action trying to get pictures of our players, and upended by the impact, she experienced a concussion from the violent hit. To make matters worse, the officials marked off the penalty, called it a second-down, and refused to talk with me about yet another error.

I have diagnosed myself with *situational Tourette's* since a few times in my coaching endeavors I have said things for which I have no idea from where they came. Well…a *situation was at hand*, and I found myself walking onto the field screaming at the head official. Eventually, I threw my visor at him. I didn't realize until we watched the film that I was literally in the middle of the field during this episode. Needless to say, flags were thrown because of my outburst, and we went from a manageable second-down to an unprecedented second-and-40 and were backed up to our 10-yard line again. I also witnessed on film that during my tirade, offensive linemen, Ethan Cleve, and Paul Carbone, were beating their chest like gorillas ready to go to battle. My stupidity somehow engaged their inner animal-like instincts. "We are all nuts" was my post-game conclusion.

Our cameraman at the time was Pete Becker who was an extremely loyal man with a knack of filming the game like a feature film cameraman. He would find things of interest on the sideline or in the stands and film it between plays. I always got a kick out of his unique shots in the middle of a highly structured game. On this night after the whole sideline episode, Pete pointed the camera to the night sky where a full moon was shining brightly between some clouds. I've since come to believe it was a perfect representation of the craziness that had occurred.

Rest in peace, Pete, you were a TRUE MARINER.

The penalty forced us into a terrible situation we could not overcome. The game subsequently proceeded with touchdowns from each side and the final scoreboard read Saints 43—Mariners 33. St. Clair rushed the field and the coveted Bell Trophy belonged to the Saints for the next year. With the win they also became MAC Gold champions for 2013. During the post-game handshakes, I gave head coach, Bill Nesbitt, a hug and congratulated him on a great game. Our kids headed immediately into the locker room, devastated.

Failure can be a productive event
if you take the time to dissect all the variables
that led to the occurrence.

Coach Bob would always say "Win or lose...take 24 hours to digest, then watch the film and evaluate your game." Post-game win or lose I always gave coaches the opportunity to address the team, and this message was the common thread. We knew our season was long from over and we had a decision to make. We could sulk in our failure, or we could rise to new levels of excellence by correcting mistakes made in the St. Clair game.

I challenged the team to make corrections, adjust, and attack the game with a new and stronger dedication. "This loss, if addressed correctly, can *be the greatest thing to happen for our team."*

"Let's not allow this loss to be a negative for too long," Captain Kevin Fitzsimmons challenged a few players who had teared up. "What are you crying for? We have a lot of games left to play."

I also addressed my sideline behavior and became emotional. "No matter what happens you should never lose your composure," I stated and pointed to my behavior as the turning point of the game. "We all need to do better, and I promise you I will work harder than ever to make this right." It wasn't the first time I had done something in coaching I regretted, but I have learned rather than dwell on anything too long, simply to take full responsibility and move on. Most fans in the community recognized my sideline actions as a fight for my beloved team and were supportive, but there was one member on the East China Schools administrative team who found my behavior unacceptable.

11

THE THREE STAGES OF EMOTION FOLLOWING A LOSS.

THE EXPERIENCE OF losing had become a rare emotion in the Mariner football program. From the year 1999 to 2012 the program experienced just 20 losses in a 14-year stretch which equates to an average of 1.4 losses per year. As I experienced setbacks during my career, I consistently observed a sequence of emotions that would run their course following a loss.

DEPRESSION sets in almost immediately and zaps you of any energy and desire for social interaction. It was crucial for the coaches to be together, following a loss, and work through this emotion congruently; alcohol was usually the catalyst for the necessary transition. The post-game parties following a loss tended to be much smaller compared to a win and would have a limited group of people attending. We only wanted to be around people who experienced the same gut-wrenching feeling. By the end of the night, the funeral parlor atmosphere would lighten; laughter and sarcasm would eke its way into the air.

Depression would leak into the following morning and there it would remain until I watched the game film. As soon as I witnessed the mistakes made, which led to the loss, the emotion of depression quickly converted to ANGER.

"Film don't lie," is a cliché that coaches use and watching this game film I noticed one mistake after another, and it created a simmering pot of consciousness within my body. I don't know how many times watching a film I had to get up and move away from the TV or computer or risk the demolition of the very technology I was using to evaluate the game. That ANGER remained until the coaches got back together on Sunday night to discuss the game plan for the next opponent and discuss any changes that needed to be addressed during the week.

We met at Coach Bob's house and at Coach Scar's house when they were head coaches. When it became my turn, we met in my classroom at the high school. I would order pizza and have some pop on hand for the meeting. It was during these coaching meetings I personally would transition to the final emotion following a loss and that was EXCITEMENT!

I would become excited in the notion that errors could be corrected in the player's practices and the Mariners could improve and become a better team following the loss. It was during this coaching meeting on the Sunday following the St. Clair loss I learned that our Superintendent at the time found my behavior during the game to be unprofessional and approached my Athletic Director about terminating me at the end of the season. This Superintendent had never coached a major sport and had little knowledge of the intensity that is experienced on the sideline during a heated game. The Athletic Director, Chris Ming, was a young first time AD but handled the situation like a veteran. He mentioned to the Superintendent that I had a long successful career in coaching at Marine City and that one incident should not lead to termination. He laid out all the potential fallout that could occur from such a move and told the superintendent he would not approve the request.

Mondays are always interesting following a loss, and on this particular Monday I wanted to find our Principal, Suzanne Cybulla, and assure her that future outbursts on the sideline would be contained. I was walking through the staff lounge toward her office when I ran into her grabbing a cup of coffee. "Suzanne, I wanted to let you know that my behavior Friday was out of line, and I promise you I will do a better job of containing my emotions." The response she gave was one that surprised me and literally made my jaw drop.

She quickly stated, "Don't apologize, I love the passion you have for the game and for your kids—he has no idea what it is like to coach in that environment."

Whatever loyalty and support I had for Suzanne Cybulla at the time was magnified tenfold by that statement. Suzanne's father was a high school football coach who also attended some of our games, and she was a former athlete who loved football. Suzanne was new to Marine City High School in 2013 and I had little experience with her, but the support she provided meant the world and created the foundation for one of the best teacher/principal relationships I would experience in my 32-year career.

Great principals and assistant principals are critical to the long-term success of any sports program. The good ones realize that teachers who coach need to be a priority when hiring for vacancies, and at Marine City we were fortunate to have a run of administrators who shared this belief. Principals like Ken Wingate, Gary Miller, Bob Rood, and Bill Jedlhe were all incredibly supportive of athletics and made it common practice to hire teachers who also coached. Assistant principals/athletic directors like Jerry Warkentien, Mike Alley, Dave Seddon, Kevin Rhien, Kevin Miller, Shannon Griffin, and Chris Ming understood the importance of athletics to the Marine City community and worked hard to upgrade our facilities and make sure our programs were adequately funded. Current administrators Sheri Becker and Dave Mroue continue to carry the same torch. I can honestly say that the administration at Marine City was a blessing and whenever we swapped stories with other coaches, we would be blown away by the lack of support they received for their schools.

As head coach, priority number one on this Monday was to get a feel for the team's temperature on that day. I would be visible in the hallways and make sure I was consistent with my friendly greetings when I saw a player. I noticed many kids avoided eye contact with me following a loss, as if they thought I was angry with them. By staying consistent with friendly greetings in the hall, I believed this helped our players understand the process involved following a loss and distracted them from any personal concerns of failure.

During our first week of practice in 2013, I made a point of stressing eye contact and handshake greetings when seeing a coach or teammate for the first time that day. With the explosion of social media and the reliance of the cell phone, I noticed kids making less and less eye contact during conversation, and I wanted to address that. The beauty of becoming a head coach during the tail end of my career was that I could focus on developing the entire student/athlete. Had I been younger, I may not have given that any thought. I am proud to say that today whenever I see a former athlete in a restaurant or out and about, the norm is that they will come over with their hand extended and say, "Hello." That this emphasis has endured for years after athletes have moved on from our program, speaks to doing things the right way and seeing those skills transfer to adulthood.

Also, in 2013 I wanted to get on board with the Facebook phenomenon and helped by some incredibly supportive moms, enhanced the Marine City Mariner Football Fan Club page. Before the season, I posted some bios of our coaching staff and some video clips of teams from the past. During our summer workouts I would post videos of kids in action, and during our camps I would post the top play of the day. It became a great way to recognize members of the program who were not as visible as the coaches on the sideline. The community was able to feel connected to the program through an effective tool that provided an up-close look at the next Mariner team. Additionally, it became a great marketing tool for fundraising efforts or merchandise sales. I am proud to say that at the time of this writing, this Facebook page has over 3,000 followers who are exceptionally loyal.

Another memorable moment occurred when Scott Whiting, of Big Dog Media, asked if he could contribute to the Facebook page. Scott's son, Justin, was an outstanding lineman for us on our 2007 State Championship team, and together they dabbled in the social media video world. Scott and Justin filmed individual interview videos of all the coaching staff and posted them to our page. Parts of our practice were filmed and used to create a hype video for the upcoming season. The father-son duo made a point to always come to our first live hitting practice and film our traditional OKLAHOMA DRILL. This drill basically pits two offensive players against two defensive players with a running back carrying the ball in a tunnel set up with agile bags. The drill brought out the intensity in the team and was great footage for the hype videos created. Scott would film games from the stands and produce a highlight film for each game he later posted to the Facebook page. A year-end highlight film was created to sell, from which 100% of the profits were donated to the program. Scott volunteered his services from the time Justin played in 2007 until I retired in 2019. As we say, Scott Whiting was and still is a TRUE MARINER.

One norm of coaching is that you're only as good as your last game. On that Monday following the St. Clair loss the Mariner Fan Page had a few comments about our coaches being out coached! The comments actually didn't bother me as I had concluded early in my career that the only opinions that mattered were the people in my inner circle who I respected. If

Coach Bob, or Coach Scar had told me I was out coached, I would have taken that to heart and looked for some immediate changes. As a veteran coaching staff, we knew that a few things needed to be addressed but there was no need to panic after losing to an excellent team. The negativity on Facebook helped create a chip we would ride for the rest of the season. Coach Bob always said, "The time to be hard on a team is after an ugly win, not after a hard-fought loss." Week 9 of the 2013 season was where our process would be reinforced and strengthened—not a week for drastic changes because playoffs were on the horizon, and, after all...we were motivated to make the long run.

12

NEXT MAN UP PHILOSOPHY.

"**YOU'RE ONE INJURY** away from being a starter, and you must practice like that injury is going to happen," was a statement we would make multiple times throughout the year to our back up players. Going into Week 9 against Port Huron Northern we had a few injuries, and we sat a few kids and let them heal up for the playoffs. Jarett Mathison (out with a knee injury) would sit out and that meant Trevor Quandt on offense and Jake Shermetaro would take his spot-on defense. Port Huron Northern created other problems for us because they were a big school with some large physical players in their lineup.

Our week of practice was uneventful—I simply wanted to get through this game and become re-energized for a playoff run. Football is a long season, and it is a grueling grind, and we were in late October, with the season having started in early August. I knew a demanding week of practice after the St. Clair loss would do more harm than good. I had great faith in our senior leadership and in our captains and let them create the accountability needed for this final regular season game.

An example of this leadership would occur when mistakes were made in practice. Instead of yelling I would calmly state, "Leaders you have 30 seconds to fix this problem, or we run." The leaders would gather around the offending party and reteach or correct the mistake in their own language. Another example played out at the end of practice where I would allow the captains to do the bulk of the talking in our wrap up huddle. Kevin Fitzsimmons and Pete Patsalis specifically shined in these moments, as they both had maturity well beyond their years.

The game opened with Northern taking the opening kickoff and putting together a 10-play drive to score and convert the extra point. 7-0 Northern with 8:52 on the clock. On our first possession we fumbled and gave the ball right back to Northern. There was an immediate buzz on the coaches' headphones, "Shit! Maybe we're not that good and its finally catching up to us."

After the fumble we forced a turnover on downs and got the ball back on our own 30-yard line. On the second play of this drive, Tate Sapienza ripped off a 46-yard touchdown run-off tackle and Olivia converted the extra point to make the game 7-7.

One mistake I made in game planning for Northern was to get away from our bread and butter 40-SERIES RUNNING ATTACK. Our evolved Wing-T offense is based on double teams and trap plays that use multiple backs and deception. Alex Merchant transferred from Northern, and I thought their coaching staff and some of their players were unfair to him. Alex transferred to the Mariners because his dad bought a funeral home in Marine City. It had nothing to do with his feelings about playing for Northern. I tried to do things with Alex to make him shine in this game, but the opposite happened. Alex was 0-6 passing and threw an interception on our second drive. Our offense was out of rhythm without Jarett, and it seemed we had lost some confidence after the St. Clair loss. We had a punt blocked, which led to a Northern score—and we looked sloppy on both sides of the ball.

What put me over the edge during this game was when offensive center, Josh Albo, experienced leg cramps on a play that ended near our sideline. He screamed in intense pain and his legs splayed out on the field at right angles to the sideline. His body was out of bounds on the sideline, but his legs remained on the field. It looked like a scene from the *Wizard of Oz* when the wicked witch was pinned under a falling house and all you could see was her legs. Being the compassionate soul I can be during a game, I told two players, "Grab his wrists and drag his ass over to the bench area." Josh was back in the game two plays later, and fortunately, his pride was hurt more than his legs.

We decided early in the second quarter to stay in two tight end formation for the remainder of the game and run the ball with passion.

---

*During halftime we challenged the offense to
use their physicality to outplay Northern.
We challenged them to send a message to
future playoff teams.*

What transpired was an incredible performance by our offensive line, which ultimately led to Tate Sapienza (203 yards rushing/3TD's), Trevor Quandt (178 yards/2TD's), and Pete Patsalis (72 yards/1TD)—all on the ground. Offensive lineman, Griffin Lictawa, gave Kenton Rivard a break this game. Together with Paul Carbone, Kevin Fitzsimmons, Ethan Cleve, Josh Albo, Dana O'Rourke, and Jake Rueter...this line dominated the line of scrimmage and churned out 470 yards of total offense. I thought this was a turning point for the mentality of our offensive unit: they believed no one could stop them, and you could see evidence on film of them blocking to the whistle like never before.

On the defensive side, Jake Shermetaro quickly gained confidence with five tackles and an interception. Joe Mazure at safety led the team with nine tackles and was by far the most underrated athlete on this team. Time and time again Joe was in the right spot—making the right plays—but because of his humble nature, and his calm demeanor, the papers rarely noticed him.

We walked off the field at Port Huron Northern with mixed emotions. Our quarterback had his worst game of the year, and our best running back was injured, but our offensive line was performing better than ever. Defensively we had given up some long drives, but we were playing a much more physical game than we had earlier in the year.

One thing we knew would happen as we entered the playoff portion of the season was that our weaknesses would be exposed quickly by the competition we were about to face. Playoff time was now upon us, and the Mariners and the community had several traditions tied to the state playoffs.

13

Playoff Time...
Playoff Traditions.

Selection Sunday dinner...

They walked into the Riviera restaurant one by one or sometimes in groups. Most were trying to avoid eye contact and most had a guilty smirk on their face. They were all Marine City football players attending the Sunday night dinner for the *Selection Sunday* show on Fox Sports, and they were all going public with their new *playoff haircut*. The show was a spinoff of the *Selection Sunday* show for March Madness and college basketball. It would present the playoff pairings for the state tournament that would start on the upcoming Friday, November 1, 2013.

The coaches told no one to do it, so it was a tradition solely created by the players, for the players. When it started, I am not sure, but the 2007 state championship team wore the cut during their historic run. The haircut style of choice for Mariner football players going into a playoff run was the easily identifiable streamlined Mohawk. It was a haircut an amateur could attempt but most players relied on their mom's or Coach Osterland's wife, Chris, to give them THE CUT. Mrs. Osterland was a loyal Mariner supporter and helped with concessions, merchandise sales, or 50/50 ticket sales. Another shining example of the great support received and needed to make the program excel.

Angelo Patsalis and his wife, Mary Beth, are the owners of the Riviera restaurant in downtown Marine City. Their oldest son Pete was a captain on the 2013 team, and they graciously offered to host the SELECTION SUNDAY DINNER. Fifty-plus Mariners crowded into the back room of the restaurant and all tables allowed a view of the TV situated high on the wall. It is a tradition that continues today, which clearly illustrates the community support for our program and the immense generosity of the Patsalis family.

WHERE IS...

Coach Bob led the Mariners in the playoffs 13 out of his 18 years as head coach. Somewhere in that time he started a tradition that occurred while the players were stretching at the beginning of practice. Coach Bob would scream at the top of his lungs (with a healthy pause between every word) "Where—is—Algonac?" The players were conditioned to scream back at the top of their lungs, "Home!" Any team from the area that had not qualified for the playoffs, or were just recently eliminated from the playoffs, was fair game. It is a tradition that still occurs today.

TO THE BEACH...

In 2013 Coach Andy Scheel joined our teaching and coaching staff at Marine City after spending 13 years at Clintondale High School. Andy was a breath of fresh air to our coaching staff, which was ageing quickly, and at times relied on yelling as the sole motivator. At Clintondale, Andy worked with many *at-risk kids* and created various tactics to encourage student athletes. Andy challenged the 2013 team at the start of the playoffs to bring home some championship hardware—district, regional, and state champion trophies. He promised that every time the Mariners would win a trophy, he would jump in the frigid St. Clair River on the following Monday.

BRING UP THE YOUNG BUCKS...

Coach Bob thought the best or most deserving JV players should be brought up to varsity for the playoffs. It was a win/win situation as the coaches would get an excellent view of the younger players' abilities and the younger players would get a firsthand look at the pace and intensity of varsity football. I always felt that having the younger team members *play up* during the playoffs was an immediate injection of energy and enthusiasm into our practices. These athletes were so excited to be on the varsity that the *eagerness to please* mentality oozed out in all directions. Coaches would also use the younger players to help with the scout teams, which would free up varsity players for more reps during scrimmage time. Finally, it was a great accountability tool for the JV coaches. They could say during the season, "If you miss practices, the varsity guys will not bring you up for playoffs."

TEAM DINNERS...

Before the Mariners even got to the playoffs, the tradition of Thursday night team dinners was already well established. I am not sure when the practice started, but it has grown to meals that are very well-planned. Over the years, several of our parents generously contributed time and money to this tradition. The players looked forward to the event so much that Thursday pre-game practices became very crisp, knowing that any sloppiness could lead to extended practices. Sometimes we would travel to a family's home and would talk about appropriate behavior when stepping into someone's home, or the families would rent out the Lion's Club, which is literally right next to our practice fields. Regardless of location, this was another opportunity to carry over life lessons from the field and into everyday life. This tradition remains in play today.

The players were done with dinner and waited for the show to progress to the Division 4 pairings. The coaching staff had a rough idea of who in our area would be possible first-round match ups, but the state selection committee always seemed to throw a curve ball in the pairings. We also traditionally were one of the last districts mentioned as the pairing started in the upper peninsula and worked its way down the west side of the state, across the bottom half of the state, and finally up the east side where Marine City is located. I, personally, would get a huge adrenaline rush from the announcement even though we were 80-90% sure who we were about to face.

We watched as the announcers discussed the pairings, the screen flashed the District 4 Pairings—and there we were!
The Mariners of Marine City in Round 1 of the 2013 state playoffs, matched up with the Vikings of Marysville.

The Mariners were the number one seed in that district with Richmond in the number two slot, Chandler Park in the three slot and the Vikings number four. Because we share a stadium, it was St. Clair's turn to choose which night they wanted for a home game (Friday or Saturday), and they chose Friday. The Mariners were scheduled to take on Marysville in a Saturday evening game—November 2, 2013, at 7:00 p.m.

SCOUTING...

Scouting opponents during the regular season had become a rare experience with the advent of Hudl, which was a video storage tool that allowed coaches to share game film with the click of a button, and greatly reduced the need to go out and see or video an opponent. With our playoff game scheduled for Saturday night, this gave our coaching staff the ability to have time to view our next potential opponent. After Friday's pre-game practice we would load up in my Durango, Coach Osterland's van, or Coach Letson's Suburban. We would head to a Coney Island style restaurant that was near the opponent's field and have dinner. The friendly banter and the ensuing laughs were wonderful medicine for the weary coaches. Luckily, our fundraising efforts allowed me to pay for everyone's dinner, which was greatly appreciated by the men.

The unity of the coaches always seemed to improve after every scouting trip, and in 2013 we took scouting to the next level. I insisted we stop on the way home at a local Big Boy® and order some pie and coffee. It was a selfish gesture at first because I loved Big Boy, but as the playoff run continued, other coaches would chime in, "Are we stopping at Big Boys tonight, Coach G?"

"You don't mess with tradition," was my immediate response.

Some have said that you might spend more time with your coaches and players during the season than with your own family. This was true for us, and I can honestly say that the guys on our coaching staff were guys I genuinely loved being around, and these scouting trips allowed us to have a brief window of calm before every intense playoff game. Longtime volunteer, Chet Wojcik, would join the scouting trips, and this was a joy for me. Chet was a great mentor early in my career and had a way of making me laugh. "Strawberry pie and coffee," was my go-to order. Bring on the Vikings!

THE BLACK SWARM.

"THE TWO-WHISTLE DRILL." If you ask any former Mariner from the past 25 years, they will tell you what the BLACK SWARM DEFENSIVE DRILL involves. It was a drill that Defensive Coordinator, Tony Scarcelli, brought to Mariner football in the mid-90s, and Tony learned of the drill from a group of Canadian football coaches we had befriended. In 1990 we struggled to find a non-league game for Week 4 of our season. Marine City is an international border town with only the St. Clair River separating the town from Canada. For years, a ferry service took passengers across the river during the summer months. Most Canadians in the surrounding Sarnia area knew about Marine City and would often visit our downtown restaurants and stores. We contacted a few schools in Sarnia to check on their interest in playing Marine City in this open slot and Dave Greenwood, the head coach of Sarnia's St. Patrick's high school responded, and just like that—a game was scheduled. The Canadians would play by American rules in this match up, simply removing one of their players on offense and one on defense.

This coaching friendship continued to grow, and Coach Greenwood invited the Mariner staff to work at an overnight football camp he ran in a campground north of Sarnia. The Mariner staff would coach half the campers and the staff from Birmingham Brother Rice (led by the legendary Al Fracassa), would coach the other half of the campers. Coach Greenwood advertised to the Canadian athletes that they would be coached by two of the best staffs in Michigan! During this camp, many ideas were shared between all the coaches and the TWO-WHISTLE DRILL was uncovered.

The drill was part of our team defense session in practice. It was activated when we would run scout offense at our starting defense. When a play was run, the first whistle would occur when the initial ball carrier or receiver was stopped, the rest of the defense then had roughly three seconds to get to that same spot on the field before the second whistle would blow. If all eleven members of the defense failed to get to that initial spot, the entire defense would face down-ups or sprints as punishment. The phrase, "Get to the ball, get to the ball," would be heard countless times during team defense, and as the team improved on this Pavlovian conditioned response, it appeared as if a Black Swarm of defenders would follow the ball.

In the opening round playoff matchup with the Marysville Vikings, the TWO-WHISTLE DRILL was put to the test like never before and the benefits of the drill shined brightly on East China Stadium and the Mariners.

The starting defensive unit that day consisted of Alec Adams and Dennis Fitzsimmons…both at defensive ends. Deep in the trenches were our defensive linemen: Kyle Scharnweber, Scott Steinmetz, and Kevin Fitzsimmons. We were blessed with linebackers, Eddie Crampton, and Jacob Headlee, who protected the middle, while corners, Tanner Star and Pete Patsalis, defended the edges. Finally, safeties, Joe Mazure, and Jarrett Mathison, were our last line of defense. On this night, the defense responded several times with big plays that turned the tide of a *win or go home* playoff matchup.

In Marysville's opening drive, the Mariner defense created piles that slowed down (1,000 yard back—#35), Brandon Stevenson, and linebackers, Eddie Crampton, and Jacob Headlee, who flowed freely to make tackles. The Vikings punted on fourth-down, but the Mariner offense failed to move the ball and gave it right back to Marysville. It was on the Vikings second drive that their quarterback (#4), Josh Smith, put on a show. The Vikings quickly transitioned to a shot gun offense, which gave Josh room to scramble. On several occasions Josh looked like Fran Tarkington, Michael Vic, and Kyler Murray as he scrambled untouched for several seconds.

The Vikings put together a time-consuming drive with the help of a Mariner 15-yard face mask penalty and scored on a halfback wheel route into the corner of the end zone. Marysville failed on the two-point conversion and was up 6-0 with just 1:52 left in the first quarter. In high school football, the first team to score wins the game nearly 70% of the time, and in this heightened playoff environment a negative mindset can be fatal.

I remember an emotional Alec Adams coming to the sidelines and expressing concern, "Coach, I can't catch him!" I reminded him of the two-whistle drill and encouraged him, "Just keep chasing and trust your teammates." Emotion plays a huge roll in playoffs and if not handled constructively, this mindset can paralyze a team. Being a veteran coaching staff, Coach Pollack, Osterland, Scheel, and Frendt sat down with the defense and reiterated the specifics that made the Mariner defense successful. The theme the defensive coaches were selling was, "Let's just keep getting 11 guys to the ball and things will work out!"

On the Mariners next drive, the ball was fumbled on the second play and Marysville recovered near midfield. The first quarter ended with the score 6-0 and Marysville on the move. Another theme the coaches sold during the playoffs was the idea of NEXT PLAY. We stressed to our players that no play should linger in their mind, and that focus needs to shift immediately to the next play. Good play, bad play, it doesn't matter...just the next play! The focus needs to shift continually to keep the mind in the right place, and as the game shifted to the second quarter, the Mariner defense was definitely tested. The swarming Mariner defense forced a three-and-out series—Marysville punted, and Marine City took over on their own 15-yard line.

Offensive coordinator, Daryn Letson, unleashed some aggressive play calling and quarterback, Alex Merchant, hit Pete Patsalis on two big pass plays to get the Mariners across midfield and into Viking territory. With the defense on their heels, Coach Letson then called a fullback trap to Jarett Mathison who raced 20 yards for our first score. Olivia was good on the extra point and the scoreboard read 7-6 with 8:53 remaining in the second quarter.

The Vikings put together another long drive, mixing power runs and scrambling quarterback escapes, to go back on top 14-7 with 4:35 remaining in the second quarter. The Mariners answered that score in just three plays, with Jarett racing 50 yards in two of them. Critical blocks by Griffin Lictawa, Kenton Rivard, Josh Albo, and Tate Sapienza led Jarett to the end zone, and Olivia again converted the extra point. The scoreboard read 14-14 with 3:56 remaining in the second quarter.

On the Vikings next possession, they gambled on fourth-down and chose not to punt. They were having a huge success running a power play-off tackle and their star running back (#35), Brandon Stevenson, was having a great game. Coach Pollack assumed the same play was coming and inserted Kenton Rivard into the defensive front to create a pile at the point of attack. Defensive end, Dennis Fitzsimmons, crashed hard off the edge and met the ball carrier with a loud *thump*. The ball shot out of the collision and linebacker, Eddie Crampton, scooped the ball and headed toward the end zone.

With the two-whistle drill employed, several Mariners ran with Eddie to create a convoy of blockers to the end zone. Safety, Joe Mazure, was out in front of the convoy and collided with the Marysville quarterback who cleared the final path for Eddie to score. It was a defensive player's dream to score on a turnover and the Mariners celebrated with great enthusiasm. The celebration was short-lived—Kenton Rivard remained on the field clutching his knee. Kenton was our dominant offensive lineman and was a great situational defensive player; he would be an enormous loss for the Mariners. The Mariners went into halftime with a 21-14 lead.

One benefit of transitioning into a two-platoon team during practice was to get more repetitions to our back up players. We were confident at halftime that back up, Griffen Lictawa, was ready to play at a high level in place of Kenton Rivard.

The Mariners kickoff return known as the STARBURST succeeded in past games with Marysville. As a result, the Vikings implemented a squib kick on each of their kickoff attempts. This resulted in the Mariners taking over at midfield nearly every time, and this was the case as the second half began. On the second play of the drive, Tate Sapienza raced 42 yards off-tackle on a play led by Griffin Lictawa. Olivia converted, and the Mariners were up 28-14 with just one minute expired on the clock.

Threating to score, midway through the third quarter, Marysville again mounted a nice drive to the Mariner 14-yard line. Quarterback, Josh Smith, booted out to the right and escaped Alec Adams. Close behind was a swarming Eddie Crampton who contained the QB and swiped at the ball. Alec, trained in two-whistles, continued to pursue and was in perfect position to scoop the ball. He returned the fumble up field 25 yards before being tackled. I clearly remember thinking, *If Alec quits on the play or pouts because he was juked again, this turnover never happens.*

Having the ball near midfield, Coach Letson agreed to one of my favorite *sudden change* traditions. As offensive coordinator, following a turnover I loved to take a shot deep on first down, so that is exactly what we did. Alex connected with a perfectly thrown ball to Pete Patsalis down the Marysville sideline where he raced toward the end zone—eventually tripped up at the three-yard line. We scored two plays later and Olivia converted, making the score 35-14 with five minutes left in the third quarter.

Much to Marysville's credit they continued to battle and put together another nice drive on offense. They crossed midfield and when faced with another fourth-down and short scenario...went for it again. The team ran the same off-tackle play which had brought success all game long and (#35), Brandon Stevenson, broke through the line of scrimmage at the 40-yard line untouched and sprinted toward the end zone. Jarett Mathison was near the Mariner sideline guarding one of their wideouts. As a two-way player, Jarett rarely came off the field but had been conditioned with our two-whistle training. Jarett chased after Stevenson as he made a beeline for the end zone, displaying a gear we rarely witnessed during practice.

Just as Stevenson was about to reach the goal line, Jarett delivered a hammer chop to (#35's) arm. The ball popped out at the one-yard line and rolled through the back of the end zone. The referees signaled a touchback, and the Mariners took over on their own 20-yard line. In my 30-plus years of coaching this may be the greatest defensive effort I have ever witnessed; the two-whistle drill and our defensive coaching staff's commitment to enforcing it should be credited.

The Vikings scored another touchdown late in the game and the final scoreboard read 35-22 in favor of the Mariners. I have witnessed many games, but I don't recall a game where turnovers and the two-whistle drill played a bigger role in the outcome. "Film don't lie" is a phrase we use in the film room following a game, and the Mariner coaching staff celebrated the several examples of the BLACK SWARM and the defensive pursuit. I also fervently believe that positive reinforcement is the strongest motivator we have as coaches, and it was our pleasure to shower our defense with encouragement. However, when praising young men there are several potential side effects and as we headed into Week 2 of the playoffs those side effects reared their ugly head.

15

THERE IS A FINE LINE.

RISK TAKING IS something I have never shied away from. As offensive coordinator for Coach Bob and Coach Scar, taking risks was the main reason I enjoyed play-calling. In 2013 when I was head coach of the Mariners, I took coaching risks several times, even knowing the outcome was always unpredictable.

As the season started, I thought it was important for this young team to see their coaches equally hard on the captains as they were on any other member of the team. If they witnessed hard coaching being thrown at the captains and saw the captains respond appropriately and constructively, then they would follow suit without hesitation. I had an idea, and I gathered the captains together at the beginning of a hot August practice.

"Now listen, this is a test of your loyalty...if anything is shared outside this circle then I know you can't be trusted. In a minute I am going to scream at you and get in your shit like never before, and you're going to just stand there and take it.

111

When I am done screaming, you will take your place at the front of the stretch lines, and you will get this practice started with some fire in your eyes."

I could tell there was a little confusion in their eyes, but I wasted no time and when my voice intensity jumped 100 decibels, they were startled, and their eyes peeled wide open. "I don't care what you want, we are going to do things my way or you can just turn your shit in. We are going to do things the right way and that is going to happen whether or not you are here. Just shut your damn mouths and do your job!" I turned and walked away and noticed 50 helmets all looking toward the captains...awaiting their response. The captains returned to the front of the stretch lines and began counting chants of each stretch.

"Right over left, down 1,2,3," Pete Patsalis shouted, and all 50 team members joined in on the count. There were no slackers—all 50 were engaged, all 50 were loud, all 50 were focused, and this risk produced the desired results.

Years later, when discussing this particular episode with the captains, they shared their memories of the event. Pete admitted, "When you started yelling, Coach, I thought *ok...this is what you mean*, and, Coach, even though you told me it was coming, I still shit my pants!"

They shared that the only team member who questioned the exchange was the *sneaky smart* senior offensive lineman, Paul Carbone. "He called bullshit right away," commented Pete.

I remember attempting to do the exact same thing with the captains of the 2018 team. It was later in the season and the wind was blowing hard on that day, so I had to yell even louder. The yelling created a spike in my blood pressure and caused my brain to experience a red out. I dropped to my knees after the exchange, and momentarily blacked out. The captains were already jogging back to their stretch lines and did not witness me on my knees, but my straight-shooting friend, Daryn Letson, saw the whole thing. "That didn't look right," he calmly commented.

"I know, I passed out for a second," I shared with Daryn as I spoke quickly, panted like a dog, and acted as if it was a normal occurrence.

"That's amazing," he said in disgust, shook his head side to side, and walked away.

Fast forward...Week 2 of the playoffs in 2013 and our rematch from the season opener with the Richmond Blue Devils. We lost twice to Richmond in 2012 and the team had taken us to the wire in the opener of 2013. We had our hands full for another four-quarter war and needed a great week of preparation. As we took the field for the start of practice on Tuesday, I sensed a general lack of focus from the team. Excessive chatter in the stretch lines, laughter in multiple areas, conversations having nothing to do with football—all created a *nail on the chalk board* sensation in my body. As if a volcano were bubbling in my feet and working its way up my body, the anger grew to where I could not contain it. "Get the f**k off this field and don't come back until you're ready to practice. Get your ass in the softball bleachers and sit there until you're ready to practice. You have 20 seconds to get all your lazy asses in those bleachers. Run, run—mooooove—now!"

I didn't give the other coaches a heads up and I didn't know the words would explode out of my mouth. Much like Tourette's, one of my many characteristic flaws are these untamed bursts of verbal anger. Unfortunately, an older couple walked on the bike bath on the south end of the practice field during the outburst. I can only imagine their thoughts as they witnessed 50 football players sprinting to the bleachers and sitting in perfect rows with their helmets on facing the softball field with no game going on.

A few minutes passed, and the team returned with a heightened focus, and we began practice. It was a highly productive practice until we got to our final session which was our two-minute offense session. We treated this session as our conditioner and wanting things to run rapidly, we needed to create fatigue in this session. With fatigue in place, we would ask the players to make many mental decisions and get accustomed to this game-like combination. Our goal during such a session was to go 80 yards of mistake-free offense and score, either by touchdown or field goal. On this day, Alex Merchant led the offense down the field perfectly until we got near the goal line. On two consecutive snaps the ball was fumbled, and the play was blown dead. Earlier in the year we would have backed the team to the starting point, and we would have made them start all over. But being in Week 2 of the playoffs and Week 11 of the season, I found this mistake inexcusable.

Turnovers can devastate a team and kill momentum in a game.

We took pride in winning the turnover battle each game and had several nuances instilled in practice to help build the mentality of ZERO OFFENSIVE TURNOVERS. One example was ball security during *run flex* at the beginning of practice. Any player who touches a ball during a game must carry a football with them during the entire *run flex* portion of pre-practice. If another player can sneak up and knock the ball out of their hands, the fumbling player must do 10 down-ups on the spot. The practice can turn into a fun game of cat and mouse as guys take pride in knocking balls free.

After the two consecutive fumbles, I was perplexed about how I should respond. I had screamed at them at the beginning of practice, so any verbal barrage at this point would be counterproductive. We were near the south end zone of the practice field, and I spotted my Dodge Durango. I parked it there daily because we would put the ball bag, the med kit and heart AED machine in the back of my car. I pulled a coaching move you can only do once a year. After the second fumble, and after the whistle blew to kill the play, I calmly walked over to the Durango parked right behind the goal post, got in, and drove away. There was no discussion with the coaches, no heads-up was given, and no emergency playbook was available to reference. I literally drove straight home, stretched out on the couch, and turned on the TV. I took a picture of my feet and the TV in the background and sent it to Daryn Letson with the caption, "Five minutes from field to couch...not bad."

Daryn responded roughly 30 minutes later, "Thanks for the heads-up, nut job! The ball bag is in my car."

We had a great week of practice the rest of the way.

16

PRESSURE IS A PRIVILEGE.

THE SONY (under the counter radio) WAS in the corner of the kitchen, under the spice cabinet. I connected my phone and pulled up Pandora radio and turned up the volume. The house was empty. The twins were both away at college and Kathy was just starting her long commute home from Novi. I had roughly one hour alone, and the sink was full of dishes. I thought, *if someone peeked in the window during one of these episodes what would they think? What would my players or coaches think of their head coach at this moment?*

Bon Jovi's *Blood on Blood* was my musical choice this cold, dark Wednesday night in mid-November. Slowly the music infiltrated my soul and parts of my body moved in rhythm to the beat. With the dishtowel over my right shoulder and the scrub brush in my right hand I began the performance. I called it *interpretative dish wash dancing with a twist of Karaoke.*

Katie, our cat, would often sit on the kitchen counter bar stool and watch the performance. The louder the better as this was no time for mellow music. Pressure is a privilege and as we entered the district championship week with the Richmond Blue Devils, this was my pressure valve. Singing, dancing, and washing dishes was my perfect medicine!

Kathy and I had become empty nesters in 2012 when the twins (Gunnar and Gabbi) embarked on their college careers. Gabbi had made the competitive cheer team at Michigan State University and Gunnar received a full tuition scholarship to Adrian college where he would play baseball. This vacancy allowed Kathy and I to eat dinner alone and it became a beautiful calming environment we both enjoyed. I would joke with my favorite secretaries at MCHS when asked, "What's it like being empty nesters?"

My canned response was, "The good news is that Kathy and I still like each other."

Kathy alone was the one person with whom I would share my true feelings. "It's tough to beat a good team twice in one season. (Richmond) I don't know if I will have Kenton this week and that is a huge loss. I don't know, Honey, if we end the season again with Richmond—the wolves are going to come out."

Kathy always had a great response, "Remember it's just a game and you're dealing with kids, not grown men so do your best to make them believe." She went on to state, "Do you realize how many times you have told me that a team is better than us and then you go out and kick their ass?" Kathy had a great way of keeping things in perspective and simplifying all the noise that sometimes-surrounded big games. I found that during the week when my mind would race with negative thoughts, I would seek her out and give her a hug. She knew her hug was a reset button for me, and it always helped me get back into the right mindset.

Richmond had stormed through their regular season undefeated after their opening loss to the Mariners. The team easily won the BWAC league championship—averaging 35 points a game—and took out Chandler Park in Round 1 of the playoffs. Leading the team were a bunch of highly talented athletes, including Jake McKiernan (linebacker/running back #1), who was 6-4 and 215 pounds, and Jake Schmidt (tight end), who was 6-6 and 230 pounds. The team was playing their best football of the year and were poised to knock out Marine City once again from the playoffs.

Playing on Saturday night allowed another huge crowd to be on hand for the district championship. We would continue to see athletes and parents from other schools who either didn't qualify for the playoffs, or were eliminated, show up to the *only show in town* game on Saturday night.

Like Marysville in Week 1 of the playoffs, Richmond scored first as (#1), Jake McKiernan, split the Mariner defense and sprinted 50 yards into the end zone. It took less than a minute for the Blue Devils to score and send a shock wave through the Mariner stands, energizing all the negative vocal buzzards. "Here we go again, Glodich. Get your head out of your ass..." came the strains of a dad with a booming voice.

On our first drive, Coach Letson leaned heavily on our offensive line and incorporated a new formation. Kenton Rivard had been fitted for a knee brace and was back in the lineup. The new formation used eight offensive linemen with quarterback, Alex Merchant, split out wide to the right and Jarett Mathison and Pete Patsalis left alone in the backfield. What is now called the WILDCAT FORMATION in college and pro football, was being run in 2013 by Coach Letson in this playoff game.

With a direct snap to Jarett, Pete would cross his face for a ball fake and Jarett would ride the fake and then head in the opposite direction. We outnumbered their defensive linemen and had great success moving the ball down the field. Jarrett would score on this drive and Olivia would convert—making the score 7-7 late in the first quarter.

Richmond answered quickly, hitting their big tight end, Jake Schmidt, on a seam route that got them down to the one-yard line. They scored on the next play and the scoreboard read 14-7 Richmond with 10:45 remaining in the second quarter. We stormed right back and got the ball down to the one-yard line but failed to score as the Richmond defense stuffed our fourth and goal attempt. The Blue Devils took over with the ball on the one-inch line.

The Mariner defense rallied round, responded, and forced Richmond to punt. Kenton Rivard, Scott Steinmetz, and Jacob Headlee aggressively combined to take away Richmond's run game. The Mariners took over on the 50-yard line and utilized a play action pass out of our FULL HOUSE T-FORMATION. At tight end, Dana O'Rourke, ran a seam route from the left side; Jarrett Mathison followed with a wheel route into the left sideline; and halfback Pete Patsalis ran a flare into the left flat area. Alex went through his progressions and saw Dana and Jarrett were well covered, leaving Pete wide open. The offensive line gave Alex all day to survey the defense, so Pete just took the pass and raced 35 yards down the Richmond sideline. Tate Sapienza scored two plays later, making a razor-sharp cutback on a sweep play, stretching to the wide side of the field. Olivia converted the extra point, and the scoreboard read 14-14, where the score remained until halftime.

On the opening drive of the second half, the Mariners utilized the growing confidence that our offensive line *could* dominate a game. Tight ends, Dana O'Rourke and Jake Reuter; tackles Kenton Rivard, Griffen Lictawa, and Paul Carbone; guards Kevin Fitzsimmons and Ethan Cleve; and center Josh Albo collectively told the coaches at halftime, "We can run the ball, Coach."

One by one these young men expressed their confidence. On a drive that comprised nine straight run plays, the Mariners marched right down the field to the Richmond 10-yard line but stalled, creating a fourth and goal from the eight-yard line. Coach Letson dialed up one of our play-action passes and Alex Merchant connected with Pete Patsalis on a corner route for the touchdown. Olivia kicked the extra point, and the scoreboard read 21-14 with 7:37 left in the third quarter.

Richmond strung together another nice drive and penetrated the Marine City 30-yard line. On a fourth and six play, Coach Pollack and the Mariner defense came up big on several levels. Defensive end, Alec Adams, picked up running back, Jake McKiernan, on a seam route; defensive end, Dennis Fitzsimmons, created pressure on the quarterback, forcing him to throw off balance; and defensive backs, Joe Mazure and Jarrett Mathison smothered the Richmond receiver, and the ball fell incomplete—turnover on downs.

We mounted a small drive and the third quarter ended with the Mariners still up 21-14 and possessing the ball around midfield. During the break between quarters Daryn asked me, "You want to do the trick play, Coach? Do-you-want-to-run-the-play?" His voice intensified with each word.

Without hesitation I responded, "Do it!" On the first play of the fourth quarter with this game still in doubt...we took a calculated risk. We split out two receivers to the left of Alex Merchant, leaving Tate Sapenzia in the back field and Pete Patsalis as a wing. Alex sent Tate in motion to the left which left an empty backfield. Alex took the snap and threw a lateral to split out receiver, Jarrett Mathison, who caught the ball roughly seven yards behind the line of scrimmage. Cole Avers and Tate Sapenzia quickly created a protection wall for Jarrett, who took a few steps forward faking a catch and run. On the third step, Jarrett pulled up and threw a pass to a wide-open Pete Patsalis, who caught the ball perfectly in stride and waltzed into the end zone.

Jarrett was an outstanding athlete who played shortstop in baseball. He possessed a strong arm and excellent hands. This skill set made him perfect for this risky game-changing play. We exploded with excitement knowing a two-touchdown lead in the fourth quarter would be tough to overcome for the Blue Devils. Olivia converted the extra point, and the Mariners led 28-14 with 11:52 remaining in the game. It was a calculated risk but we knew motion would create confusion and Jarrett could gain yards if the pass was not open. We also knew if we failed, we still had three more plays to get the first down. It was one play where the anticipation was unbearable and because it was executed so perfectly, the celebration was explosive. I have been asked many times when speaking about coaching as a profession, "Where else can you have a job where you get goosebumps and jump up and down like a kid?"

Richmond tried to counter with a trick play of their own on the ensuing kickoff. They took the kick and sprinted to the right side of the field, only to stop and throw back to a lone player on their sideline. Joe Mazure stayed in an ideal position and slowed up the ball carrier before Scott Steinmetz finished the tackle.

We traded a couple of possessions back and forth with punts before Richmond mounted their next scoring drive late in the fourth quarter. Richmond hit Jake McKiernan on a seam route to make the score 28-21 with just 3:23 remaining in the game. Jake Reuter's athletic play secured an onside kick for the Mariners around midfield, after Richmond's attempt failed. Richmond burnt us using onside kicks in 2012 as they recovered two attempts. We inserted players who were aggressive with the ball and who had good hands. Jake stepped up big during a critical time of the game.

Once again, the Mariner offensive line took over. Using a powerful I-FORMATION with linebacker, Eddie Crampton, in the backfield, the player line created huge holes for Tate and Jarrett to run through. We went into slowdown-mode and took as much time off the clock as possible between plays. Keeping the ball 100% of the time on the ground, the Mariners scored with 1:48 remaining in the game. The scoreboard read 35-21 Mariners.

Richmond quickly moved the ball down the field and got into Marine City's red zone but that's as far as they would penetrate. The game ended with pass plays being disrupted by Jake Shermetaro, Jarrett Mathison, and Pete Patsalis. The Mariners had won the district championship and after shaking hands with Richmond...lined up at midfield for the medal and trophy presentation.

Richmond displayed great class and lined up opposite the Mariners and although with tears in their eyes, applauded the presentation. We had experienced what Richmond was going through several times in the program's history and I was proud Coach Bob had instilled the character to do what is right—respect the opponent regardless of whether you won or lost the game.

In our post-game huddle with the players, Coach Osterland followed a theme he started earlier in the year, "You have won nothing yet, so don't stop working, you have won nothing!"

We shared our 24-hour rule for the 800th time—*Enjoy this for 24 hours and then get ready to work because your opponent next week is coming from a whole different world.* Country Day was on the clock, and it was a clock no one in Marine City could afford.

17

TAP, TAP, TAP.

WITH THEIR BLACK helmets on and their black home jerseys pulled over their shoulder pads, the Mariners exited the locker room and headed toward the main tunnel of the Ford Field underbelly. Two by two in formation they seemed to walk in unison, and as they turned the corner into the main tunnel, their cleats met the cement floor. Tap, tap, tap. The tunnel echoed the marching cleats as the Mariners walked the curved pathway toward the Ford Field playing surface. The grey darkness of the tunnel transitioned and as they made the final curve, the bright lights of the field beamed through the end point. When all the Mariners reached the end of the tunnel, a small buzz slowly arose from the fans on the home sideline; it strengthened as the Mariner faithful realized their hometown boys were about to take the field, and as the last Mariner exited, the sound exploded into a bona fide roar in the home of the Detroit Lions.

November 23, 2007, was considered Black Friday in the retail shopping world, but in Marine City it was considered Black Friday because the Mariners were about to play in their first state championship game against the talent-laden Detroit Country Day Yellow Jackets. In the previous week, our team had defeated the Kingsford Flivvers and became only the third team to reach that depth in the playoffs and the first team ever to advance.

During the program's history, the semifinals were reached when Jerry Warkentin's 1985 Mariners lost to eventual state champions—Dearborn Divine Child. In 1994 Bob Staskiewicz's Mariners lost to eventual state champion, Monroe Jefferson. That year's team was loaded with talent, including our first Division 1 player, Wes Kammer. Division 2 athletes, Brett Warkentien, and David Donaldson, were dominant players on that team. The team's journey was highlighted by a last-second win over Allen Park when backup quarterback, Matt Griffor, threw a desperation touchdown pass to Wes Kammer in the end zone on the game's last play. Since 1994, the Orange and Black had lost seven straight regional finals, many of those losses occurring to Catholic league power, Orchard Lake St. Mary's. Tony Scarcelli's 2007 Mariners advanced to a game that many in Marine City thought would never occur. It was a historic run and the loyal Mariner fans showed up in massive volume to display their support.

On the way out of town that day, the Mariner buses. with police and fire escort, weaved their way through the streets of Marine City—eventually landing in the downtown district.

There, the Mariner buses were greeted by fans lining the streets and flashing motivational signs. Mr. Jerry Wesley, father of fullback, Joe Wesley, stood atop his Suburban SUV waving two orange Mariner flags and wearing a huge football head. The buses were followed by a long caravan of cars that had spirit paint popping from the tinted windows of most cars. *Intimidate, dominate*, and *go-black* were some of the common phrases painted on the cars. There was even a short school bus painted all black with harpoons painted on both sides, which was magically injected into the caravan.

The support spilled over to Ford Field where a sea of orange fans filled the bottom level of seats—from goal line to goal line. Workers at Ford Field commented that it was the largest sideline attendance they had witnessed for a high school state championship game. The football players, the loyal fans and community, and the coaching staff were all in for an event that took on surreal qualities.

The Mariners had a tall task that day as they took on a team loaded not only with Division 1 talent but a team with three eventual NFL players on the roster. Receiver, Bennie Fowler, would play at Michigan State; linebacker, Kenny Demens, would play at Michigan; and running back, Jonas Gray, would go on to play at Notre Dame, before playing in the NFL. On paper, and in rational thinking, very few in the newspaper world gave the Mariners much of a chance.

Tony Scarcelli's defense was the story of the day as the undersized overachieving Mariners swarmed the ball all night and kept Country Day's offense in check and off the field.

Corner back, John Lyszczyk, at just 5-7 and 150 pounds, played like a rabid wolf that day, knifing off the edge of Country Day's offensive line and tying up Jonas Gray's legs before he ever got a head of steam going. Defensive linemen, Travis Avers, Eddie Johns and Russ Ferqueron, continued to do their dirty work. Our boys crawled…they slanted…they dove, and they tied up Country Day's offensive line, preventing any downfield. Linebackers, Mike Matyniak, and Brent Weil, and defensive ends, Shawn Duvall, and Josh Byrd, created stand ups and stalemates to add to Country Day's frustrations. Defensive backs, Matt Connin, Zach Bachler, and Steve Faucher allowed little success in their passing game and the Yellow Jacket offense produced just seven points on that day—not scoring until late in the game.

On offense, our own Division 1 talented quarterback, Brendon Kay, connected twice for touchdowns with speedy receiver, Chad Allemon. Chad's first touchdown catch remains in my mind the greatest pass and catch in Mariner history. Brent Weil, in my opinion the best tight end we ever produced, caught two passes in heavy traffic, while Joe Wesley and Jamal Abrams contributed huge offensive plays that allowed the Mariners to rack up 21 points. The offensive line, led by Steve Churhan, Justin Whiting, Robert Salsbury, Bruce Boulier, Travis Calu, Travis Osterland, and Jeremy Kierszychowski protected Brendon Kay and effectively *controlled* the line of scrimmage—especially late in the game.

When the final play occurred, and John Lyszczyk upended an outstretched Bennie Fowler—causing the ball to fall to the turf—the Mariners rushed the field with many tears of joy oozing from their smiling eyes.

The Mariners' improbable ending was one of pure joy as they became the first team in Marine City history to bring home a football state championship.

It was a vision created by Coach Bob and Coach Warkentien on the day Coach Bob was hired in 1987 and both visionary men were on the sideline to witness this game.

The Mariners would not face Country Day again until the 2013 regional final game and this game would be played outdoors on a cold Saturday night in November. The Mariners would prepare all week on the chilly turf of East China stadium, whereas the Yellow Jackets would practice all week in their warm new state-of-the-art indoor practice facility. Just one of the million differences between Marine City and Country Day. Marine City's success is built around the philosophy of the team; Country Day's success constructed from their talent.

A classic face off: team vs talent.

18

THE GREAT EQUALIZER.

THERE WERE A million differences between the football programs at Detroit Country Day and Marine City, but after March 1, 2011, there were six million more differences. On that day, the Yellowjackets opened their new indoor turf athletic facility—125 yards long and 65 yards wide. The cost of the new facility came from a private donor and totaled just over $6 million dollars. No other high school in Michigan had their own private indoor training facility, and it was a card that our coaching staff would play to our advantage all week long.

The offense run at Marine City has been described as an evolved WING-T-OFFENSE. It's not a sexy offense, it's not an offense you will see on Saturdays or Sundays on national TV or on Monday night football. The offense produces double teams at the point of attack and creates confusion with multiple fakes. As I became offensive coordinator and Coach Bob gave me ownership and freedom, I implemented multiple formations to create even more confusion. Coach Bob called the offense the *great equalizer,* which he knew was the answer to the question: "How do you beat teams with more available talent than you?"

After the district championship against Richmond, the coaches, and their wives were found in the Glodich basement, where Kathy had prepared food and was busy making the wives drinks at the bar. We hosted most of the after-game parties and one thing I loved about doing so was seeing my dad interact with the other coaches. We had converted the front office into a bedroom for Dad and if we had a home game, he would spend the weekend with us. Mom had passed away in 2005 and Dad was transitioning out of his house and would rotate between his three sons. After summer and into fall, Dad spent a great deal of time at our house, and we were lucky to have him.

Our trainer, Bob Scharnweber, called him Pops and would spend most of the night by his side. Sharny stood behind the bar as well and made sure Dad would have a couple Crown Royals throughout the night. Sharny had lost his dad and spending time with my father, I am sure, was therapeutic. They enjoyed each other's company. At the end of this particular party, our coaching staff gathered on the chairs and couches in the large portion of the basement, and we discussed the talent on the Country Day team.

In my 30-plus years with Marine City football, we were fortunate to produce three players who received Division 1 football scholarships. That is three players over 30 years at

Marine City, but this 2013 Country Day team had five players committed to play Division 1 football. The quarterback, Tyler Wiegers, was headed to Iowa; their top receiver, Maurice Ways, would land at Michigan; the best running back, Richard Wilson, would play for Boston College; their fastest player/receiver, Jacob Hill, would find his way to Syracuse; and their best offensive lineman, Justin Hunter, was headed to Harvard. The number of Division 1 offers for the Mariners in 2013 was zero—and that was the norm.

We quickly shifted from a team and coaching staff expected to win by most prognosticators—to a game that most predicted the Mariners had no chance of winning. I joked as we listed all the talented Country Day players, "Someone might get hurt this game."

Country Day was a team that was depressing to watch on film. A team loaded with talent that in turn created many matchup problems. We had faced something remarkably similar in the 2011 playoff win when we took on Detroit Crockett, who was also loaded with Division 1 talent.

Eventually, we ended the night fostering high fives and hugs and the mindset we could compete with the best of teams, and this upcoming week was just another test of that mindset. No one, and I mean no one, would tell Coach Dave Frendt and Captain Pete Patsalis they couldn't win next Saturday. Those two men embodied the competitor spirit like no one else on the team and I found it very contagious and motivating. The direct stare they would give you, the repeated nod of their head and the limited word choice, "All right, let's go," created a Rocky-IV-like-persona, which gave me fuel for the tough week ahead.

Monday's practice simply involved some light lifting in the weight room and some film study and then we headed to the track to run a mile. I ran with the kids during this playoff run and instructed them to stay behind me the whole mile. What transpired was the poor kids running the slowest mile they could ever imagine, and me dealing with fat fatigue!

After completing the mile, we headed to the Marine City beach where Coach Andy Scheel would make good on his promise to run into the freezing river after every championship trophy received. On this Monday it would only be the Mariners and Andy's parents—with warm towels in waiting—to witness the splash. The weather was brutal, and the kids were eager to witness the event and get back into their warm cars. Andy completed the splash into the frigid river and was wrapped up immediately as he exited. Any other coach on the staff would have gone into cardiac arrest with the shock to the body. Andy willingly took one for the team.

Tuesday through Friday we practiced at East China stadium where the temperatures were a true November cold. We preached that...

> Saturday night would be just as cold (Mariner weather) and we would be ready, whereas Country Day who was practicing in their nice warm indoor facility would be unprepared.

It was critical to stay even with Country Day through the early part of the game to create doubt, and that we could build on that doubt with our swarming defense and deceptive offense.

If we could get into the fourth quarter and still be within reach…talent would be thrown out the window and the will to win would overtake the mind.

At the end of Wednesday's practice, I stressed to the team, "You're going to be hit like never before, and you're going to see speed like never before, but if you can sustain and hang around, they are going to ask, 'What do we need to do?' And that's when we will take over." I reminded them of the *Rocky IV* movie and how this win would be our version of that film.

Our kids really bought into our coaching mindset, making for an amazing week of practice. Throughout the week, we kept responding to media requests for press box or sideline access. The *David and Goliath scenario* made us certain that the Mariners would have the support of the entire area and the stands would be full.

On Friday night our scouting trip took us into the heart of Lansing to watch Lansing Sexton against Saginaw Swan Valley. Lansing Sexton came out on top and was impressive in the win. At the end of the night, we ran into the Country Day coaching staff as we exited the stadium. It was crystal clear to us during our brief discussion with their staff that they were planning to play Lansing Sexton in the semifinal game.

"The semifinal game will probably be Brighton, that's about halfway," mentioned one of their coaches. He also made note, "Whoever wins tomorrow night will go to the finals." He was respectful and not condescending but said it with enough confidence and bravado to imply that they were the far superior team and perhaps overlooking us. No one in the local media predicted the Mariners going to the state finals; most writers predicted, instead, that Country Day would be. The classic stage was set, yet very few people would predict the impact a collective group could flood the stands on that Saturday night.

19

Every Stinking Time.

THEIR SIGN STRETCHED across the thick rubber runway. The runway funneled players out of the tunnel and across the track and onto the stadium turf. The stadium lights reflected the yellow and blue paint, and the white paper of the sign was offset by the pitch-black sky. It was being held by the Country Day cheerleaders as Country Day waited to run onto the field. Facing the Mariners' stands, the sign was visible to the packed crowd. On the other side of the field, only a quarter of the Country Day sideline stands were occupied. The sign read, SINK THE MARINERS.

The boys were in the locker room, and I stood outside the door. It was my ritual to wait outside the locker room to gather my thoughts and let the boys settle before I gave my pre-game speech. When the clock hit two minutes, I entered the locker room and gave the command, "Helmets on." There was no need for that statement as every single player had their helmet on and chin strap buckled. There was complete silence in that room and each player locked into my eyes and returned my intent gaze. Eye contact was a behavior we stressed during communication, and on this night their eyes spoke from the depths of their souls. From the captains who sat up front…to the JV players seated in the back of the room, their eyes glowed with intensity.

This group of men was ready to go to battle, and this group of men believed they could do the unthinkable.

The room was filled with the Mariners waiting to go to battle, but was also filled with the entire coaching staff, the eager group of water boys, our medical staff, our statisticians, and our videographer, Mr. Whiting. When addressing the team, I used a style that started off with a calm and factual voice to one that built with intensity and loudness until the very end, I repeated a statement at the top of my lungs. I reminded…

The men what I thought made them an incredible group.

Each of them about being grounded in the junior football days which they started in the fourth grade.

The squad about their experience with eighth-grade football, then JV football and all the hours they sweated together.

The team about the summer workouts, and how they would jump in the river after the workouts.

And then my voice rattled and increased in decibels with each word, "And all those experiences you have shared makes you a home-grown team...and all those experiences and pain that you have shared...makes you care about each other like you were brothers."

In my next statement I cut it loose and let it boom from my voice as loud as I could, "And on this night—and on this field—I will take TEAM OVER TALENT every time, I will take TEAM OVER TALENT every stinking time.

"Let's go!"

The boys stood, the boys roared, and the boys stormed out of the locker room and into the tunnel. Noticing the boys in the tunnel, our band director, Mr. Uhrig, played our entrance song, *Space Odyssey 2001*. With Jim Labuhn pointing the fire extinguisher toward the field, the team waited for the go ahead from Coach Frendt and when the song hit the *mark*, the Mariners poured through the extinguisher smoke and onto the field, with flag men leading the way. The Mariners stopped at the near hash mark and piled into a massive huddle with Jarrett Mathison coming out of the tunnel last, circling the huddle and leaping on top, where the boys held him momentarily.

It was game time.

After a beautiful cross kickoff from Jacob Rhein, the Yellowjackets took over on the Mariners 26-yard line and immediately took a shot deep on their first play. Pete Patsalis slipped in coverage and Country Day's best receiver, Mo Ways, ran by him and caught the ball over his right shoulder, going out of bounds for a 30-yard gain. Coach Pollock, our defensive coordinator, and Coach Frendt, our defensive back coach, had planned the utilization of movement to disguise coverages. On the next play the Mariners constantly motioned with the linebackers and defensive backs moving in all directions. This confusion, as well as Mr. Uhrig and the band playing music to the snap of the ball, forced Country Day to take a time out. Country Day was using a *check with me* offensive strategy where the coaches would signal in plays after seeing what the defense was doing. With the Mariners constantly in motion, the Country Day staff discovered new challenges, and when the quarterback finally echoed the play, our band noise was a challenge for him to scream over.

The officials came over to our sideline and instructed Mr. Uhrig to stop playing when the officials gave the *ready to play* signal. Mr. Uhrig, of course, complied but summoned the members of the Marching Band to make noise with their voices between plays. The one-hundred-strong Marching Mariners accepted the challenge and created pandemonium, forcing the Yellowjackets to take a second time out. On the Yellowjackets' next play, they went to their star running back, Richard Wilson, but a timed stunt from linebacker, Eddie Crampton, stopped Wilson in the backfield and the Black Swarm defense prevented any gain. After a few incompletions, the Yellowjackets failed on a fourth-down conversion and the Mariners took over on their own 37-yard line.

The Mariners were in their all-black home jerseys and the running backs all wore black arm pads. Another part of Coach

Bob's *great equalizer* concept was the way the Mariner running backs carried the football. The traditional style in football is under the arm pit, tucked on one side. In Marine City, since 1987 when Coach Bob first took over, running backs carried the ball with both arms in front and the ball tucked under and slightly hidden with arm pads. When done correctly and when several running backs are all doing the same thing, it becomes deceptive. Coach Letson wanted to create confusion immediately with the Yellowjacket defense, so he utilized our T-Formation and utilized multiple fakes.

What resulted in our first drive were big-chunk-plays of +10, +7, +9 (yards) and multiple first downs. Coach Letson also used a simple trick to slow down the defensive line, which was called PLAYDO. The Mariners would sprint to the line and get down and get set like normal, then quarterback, Alex Merchant, would bark his cadence, but the Mariners would not move. If the defensive line was overly aggressive, then they might jump offsides, and this happened during this first drive. The Mariners marched right down the field and with a couple of pass completions to Pete Patsalis and Cole Avers, the Mariner scored on a fullback trap to Jarrett Mathison. Jarrett went untouched as Tate Sapenzia carried out a great fake, and most of the Yellowjackets chased after him, while Jarrett snuck into the end zone. Olivia converted on her extra point and the Mariners led 7-0 late in the first quarter.

Our receivers coach, Joel Whymer, was also our boys' basketball coach, and he was in his first year of coaching football. After we scored on our opening drive, he came over to Coach Letson and myself and stated, "I think we got this."

Coach Letson and I said nothing in return but we both smiled as we reflected on his shared innocence and enthusiasm.

During Country Days' second drive, edge rusher, Alec Adams, caused a fumble they recovered. On third-down, sophomore linebacker, Jacob Headlee, put his shoulder into the exposed ribs of a Country Day receiver and forced an incompletion. Country Day was forced to punt, and the ball rolled into the end zone.

The Mariners failed to move the ball on their second possession...punting it right back to Country Day. Starting the second quarter, the Yellowjackets again took a shot deep to their Michigan-bound receiver, Mo Ways. Pete Patsalis was in perfect position but mistimed his jump to break up the pass and Mo Ways went untouched into the end zone. They converted the extra point, and the game was tied with 10:08 remaining in the second quarter.

Country Day kicked the ball deep to the Mariners where we utilized our well-known kickoff return, the Starburst. In this return Jarrett Mathison was considered the quarterback and allowed the three other backs to convene quickly and take their fakes away in multiple directions. Jarrett kept the ball and weaved his way through the Yellowjackets and was eventually brought down on the 23-yard line. This was a huge answer to Country Day's score, and the Mariners threatened to score again. Utilizing Jarrett in the WILDCAT FORMATION we created a fourth and goal scenario.

Playoff football and regular season games seem to take on a different mindset when in these short yardage situations. Our general rule in the playoffs was to take points when presented with the opportunity, but here I rolled the dice, and decided not to kick the field goal. I was confident our O-line could get us that one yard. What resulted was a great defensive push from Country Day; a failed fourth-down attempt from the Mariners. It was a decision that could have easily come back to haunt us, but I was amazed how business-like the kids and the coaches were even after the failed attempt. Coaches Pollock, Frendt, Osterland, and Scheel were immediately telling the defense, "Ok, we've got to get the ball back. Let's focus—here we go."

Country Day showed on the next drive why so many thought they were state title bound. They took over on the one-inch line and put their workhorse (#2), Richard Wilson to work. He provided punishing runs of +8, +15, +12 to get the Yellowjackets near midfield. On a third and seven-play near midfield, Country Day connected with their speedy (and Syracuse-bound) receiver, Jacob Hill, on a curl route. He broke one tackle and raced down the Country Day sideline for the score. The Yellowjackets converted the extra point and led 14-7 going into halftime.

20

THE CATCH.

THE MARINE CITY coaching staff met under the bleachers and outside the locker room during halftime. We had every reason to be upset with what transpired in the second quarter. We failed to score from the one-yard line, and we gave up a touchdown pass with under a minute to play before the half. Collectively as a group we agreed we were right where we wanted to be, and our *Rocky IV* analogy was coming to life. We would receive the ball in the second half and if we could score on that opening drive, the Yellowjackets might allow panic and doubt into their pampered minds.

We addressed the team with a calm and business-like approach and reminded them of our goal to stay close. The offensive line shared with me that they thought Country Days' defensive line was softening. "Coach we can run the ball," claimed right tackle, Paul Carbone.

"Let's go right at them, Coach," added Senior Captain and left guard, Kevin Fitzsimmons.

We discussed a fullback run play with base blocking and big splits, and we drew up the concept on the dry erase board. Our final statement to the team before we exited the locker room...

"TEAM OVER TALENT gets you to Ford Field fellas!
Don't let your brothers down, play for your
brothers and have no regrets when you come
off that field.
Let's go Black!"

On our very first play of the second half, we tried the fullback run play that utilized straight ahead base blocking with a FULL HOUSE T-FORMATION. Jarrett Mathison took the hand-off and followed a great triple team of the nose guard from Ethan Cleve, Josh Albo, and Kevin Fitzsimmons. We left the defensive tackles untouched and let them come up field unblocked. This was a calculated risk, but the speed of the hand-off and the way Jarrett attacked the hole made it a good gamble. Tackle, Paul Carbone, dipped through the defensive line and beautifully picked their play side linebacker, and tight end, Jake Rueter, sprinted downfield and got to their safety. With multiple fakes being carried out by Tate Sapienza and Pete Patsalis, the Yellowjackets did not realize Jarrett had the ball until it was too late! Jarrett raced 76 yards down the

Mariner sideline for the opening score of the second half. Olivia converted the extra point, and the game was tied up at 14-14 with 11:46 remaining in the third quarter. The Mariner sideline was quickly infused with energy and our marching band echoed the euphoria and continued to wreak havoc with the Yellowjacket offense.

After a couple of failed possessions from both the Yellowjackets and the Mariners, the game neared the end of the third quarter. At this point Country Day's (#2), Richard Wilson. seemed to be on a mission to take the game into his own hands. With a steady diet of run plays, (#2) punished any Mariner that got in his way. On an off-tackle play on this drive, Wilson (#2) ran over our gritty but under sized corner, Tanner Star. I need to give credit to Tanner—even though he was 80 pounds lighter, Tanner held on for the tackle. On the next play the ball was tossed to Richard where he broke two tackles at the line of scrimmage then escaped the grab of Pete Patsalis and eventually trucked through defensive back, Grant Sharpe, on the goal line. The score gave the lead back to Country Day, 21-14 and sent Grant Sharpe to the hospital with concussion concerns.

On our next drive we put together a couple of nice runs but stalled around midfield, where we punted. Punter and tight end, Dana O'Rourke, feathered a beautiful punt downed on the three-yard line. Having multiple scout films to study, our defensive coaches knew Country Day had a strong tendency to throw deep on first down coming out of their own end zone. Pete Patsalis relayed this to the entire secondary in the huddle. Sure enough, on first down the Yellowjackets attempted a deep ball to Mo Ways on their sideline. Pete was in the perfect position to break up the pass and deflected the ball where teammate, Joe Mazure, intercepted it and headed toward the end zone. Joe's return was short when he was stopped cold after taking a brutal hit from (#2) Richard Wilson.

On the Mariners' first play following the interception, we ran a power play called RED RIGHT 434. It is an unbalanced formation where we put both tackles side by side. In this play, tackle, Paul Carbone, down blocked much of the Yellowjacket defensive line, and tackle, Kenton Rivard, took their defensive end for a ride. Much like the scene from the movie, *Blindside*, Kenton put the end on roller skates and forced him to backpedal for 10 yards, after which Kenton finished the block by putting him squarely on his back. We refer to this successful block as a PANCAKE, and Kenton was ready for some syrup. Jarrett received the hand-off and shot through the big hole with a full head of steam. He weaved through several Country Day defenders, and as he neared the 20-yard line, (#2) Richard Wilson had Jarrett in his sites. Richard connected with Jarrett helmet-to-helmet, causing Jarrett to spin wildly and fall to the ground, where he lay on his back motionless. Chaos broke out around him.

When Jarrett hit the ground, the ball popped free, a scramble and a pile ensued with the players assuming it was a fumble. Paul Carbone was racing downfield when he noticed the fumble and jumped into the pile to recover the ball. At 6-4 and 280 pounds, Paul jumping into the pile was more like Orca the Killer Whale jumping into the splash pool at Sea World®.

When Paul landed headfirst and momentarily knocked himself silly, the officials blew the play dead and ruled it was not a fumble, saying the ground caused the fumble.

On this night, some of our medical staff were not available to be on the sideline. That left our eighth-grade coach, Scott Uppleger, and me (a mere biology major) with the most medical knowledge. Jarrett was motionless on his back, and Paul was attempting to stand up, but his legs were not responding. Cole Avers attempted to help Paul but he fell right back to the ground. He resembled a baby giraffe trying to take his first steps and failed three times in a row. At this point, I noticed the Country Day medical staff running across the field and I knew if they got to the scene, they would deem all Mariners unfit to return to play. I ran toward their medical staff with both hands up in the air yelling, "We've got this. No need for help. We've got this!" They stopped, looked surprised, and headed back to their sideline.

I directed Scott Uppleger to take Paul to the sideline and to put him through our sideline concussion protocol, while I attended to Jarrett who was still motionless on his back. When I kneeled next to Jarrett, I noticed his helmet was off, but his eyes were closed. I put my hand on Jarrett's chest and asked, "Talk to me buddy, what are you feeling? Where does it hurt?" There was an uncomfortable delay, and a million negative thoughts ran through my head.

Finally, after what seemed an eternity, Jarrett opened his eyes and said, "Coach, I am fine. I just need to rest—I just needed a break!"

A penalty was accessed to the Yellowjackets for helmet-to-helmet contact and that got us near the 10-yard line. Coach Letson used our PLAYDO again, and we got Country Day to jump offsides, moving us to the five-yard line. Then on first and goal from the five, Coach Letson called for a play action pass out of our T-FORMATION and Alex Merchant found Jarrett in the back of the end zone for our next score. Olivia converted, and the game was tied 21-21 with much of the fourth quarter remaining!

A poorly placed SQUIB KICK gave Country Day the ball near midfield. The Yellowjackets fed (#2) the ball on four consecutive runs where he rambled for one first down after another. As chaos erupted in the third quarter, #2 found more determination to take control of the game. Then, he ran eight yards to score the next point for Country Day on a left-side toss play. The Yellowjackets were back on top 28-21 with eight minutes remaining in the game.

The Mariners answered quickly, using play action passing and a huge gain from Merchant to Mathison for 53 yards. Jarrett scored another touchdown for the Mariners with the WILDCAT FORMATION. The extra point snap rolled backwards, and Olivia never got to kick the ball. This was a major mistake for the Mariners as we now trailed 28-27 midway through the fourth quarter.

Country Day returned to their punishing ground game and continued to feed Richard Wilson the ball. Consecutive runs of +12, +7, +8, +10 (yards) moved the ball into the red zone. It seemed inevitable that the Yellowjackets would score again. On a second and five play, Country Day again gave the ball off-tackle to (#2), Richard Wilson. Corner back, Tanner Star, under cut the lead blockers and popped up to tackle (#2) for no gain. The play resembled John Lyszczyk's technique in the 2007 State championship game when he made several tackles on future NFL bound, Jonas Gray. On a third and five play the Mariners stuffed a quarterback-draw, and it was on a fourth and five play that Alec Adams sacked the Yellowjacket quarterback...giving the Mariners the ball on the 30-yard line with about three minutes to play.

On our first play we put Alex Merchant out wide, put Jarrett at quarterback, and ran a multi-fake play for Jarrett over the right tackle. Jarrett raced fifteen yards for a first down, and we quickly followed with a fullback trap to Jarrett for seven yards. Tate followed with a nice run-off tackle for a first down and a 12-yard gain. We struggled to gain yardage on our next two plays and that created a third and seven with 1:33 left on the clock. We ran a hook and ladder play we had been saving, and found Pete on a curl route, who then pitched to Jarrett coming out of the back field. The play went for 13 yards and a first down, but more importantly—it stopped the clock. We got Country Day to jump offsides again, and that moved the ball down to the 18-yard line.

On second-down we called a play action pass designed to go to Pete Patsalis. Cole Avers was instructed to run at the Country Day safety and screen him from covering Pete. Richard Wilson (#2) was assigned Cole man to man on this play, and he decided the best way to do that was to bump Cole with authority. Cole was lifted off the ground, placed on his back, and never found his way to the safety, which allowed the

Yellowjackets to double cover Pete. The offensive line gave quarterback, Alex, great protection, and he could set his feet and make the perfect throw. Pete angled to the northwest corner of the end zone and got his hands on the ball just over his left shoulder. The ball deflected off Pete's hands and bounced straight up keeping its motion in line with Pete's body motion. As Pete neared the back of the end zone and the corner pylon, the ball came back down where Pete pinned the football to the front of his helmet. Pete's knee hit the end zone turf first, and he slid through the back pylon keeping the ball pinned to his helmet the whole time.

The officials hesitated on the call and converged before making a signal. After a brief meeting, the officials in unison with each other, signaled for a touchdown! What ensued was a celebration like I have never experienced before. Coach Letson and I jumped again and again like gazelles on the Serengeti plains of Africa. Coach Tony Scarcelli quickly brought us back to reality and instructed us to go for a two-point conversion. We took a time out and decided on a play—which failed—making the score 33-28 with just 45 seconds remaining in the game.

Jacob Rhein gave us a beautiful cross kick to the 18-yard line where speedy (#24) took the ball and headed toward their sideline. Tanner Star held his ground on their sideline and juked two potential blockers to make an amazing open field tackle. On the first snap, the quarterback took a deep drop to allow their receivers to go down field. Kevin Fitzsimmons fought his way through the offensive line and squarely hit the Yellowjacket quarterback in the back, causing a fumble. The thought ran rampant through our minds, *If the Mariners recover the ball the game is over,* so a mad scramble ensued.

Out of that mess came one of the huge Yellowjacket linemen running with the ball downfield. He gained 27 yards before being tackled. On the next play they quickly threw the ball out to speedy (#24) who started downfield. He elected to try for added yardage instead of getting out of bounds. Jake Shermetaro made a great open field tackle and brought him down in the playing field as the clock continued. They spiked the ball to stop the clock, and this brought up a fourth and 10 with just 10 seconds on the clock. On the last play they ran a hook and ladder themselves, eventually pitching the ball to speedy (#24). Like a video game, he wove his way through our defense, deciding several times to run backwards to create space. For a moment it appeared there was enough room on our sideline for him to make a break. A collective gasp came over the entire Mariner sideline and he picked up speed and headed downfield. Finally, the Mariners, Scott Steinmetz, and Jake Shermetaro, corralled the runner and brought him to the turf. Scott suffered a concussion on this play, as he was hit early by a lineman but got up and pursued the play and eventually made the tackle. He stayed prone in pain on the turf while the rest of us celebrated.

The Mariners had done the unthinkable—they had beaten a team loaded with Division 1 talent. A team that most media professionals were convinced would advance to the state title game. What did the Mariners receive because of this epic win? The Mariners received a match up with what most journalists were calling, "The greatest high school football team to ever come out of Lansing. The Lansing Sexton Big Reds."

21

FIRE! 15,14,13,12.

THE VISUAL CONTRAST was striking. It was as though our eyes were playing games with our minds. When we formed a huddle to prepare for an extra point attempt, there was an immediate buzz from the opposing stands. Olivia was listed on our roster as 5-2 and 118 pounds and the men assigned to protect her were slightly different, 6-2 and 210 pounds, 6-3 and 300 pounds, 6-4 and 280 pounds, and so on. Once the ball was snapped and Olivia attacked the ball, kicked it, and ran off the field, the minds would transition. "Damn she's good," is what I suspected.

"Olivia, what *was* she tonight? She didn't miss, right? She is a tough, tough football player, and if she's a girl, I don't care because she's got a football mentality." Those were my comments to multiple reporters post-game at Ford Field, when asked what I thought about my kicker.

They say necessity is the mother of invention, and in 2013 the Marine City Mariner football program had a necessity. We didn't have a reliable kicker waiting in the wings, and that was my fault. Succession planning was something that I observed from Coach Bob when I was a young coach. We had a late scrimmage every year, and it only involved underclassmen. I remember Coach Bob was always so energetic after those scrimmages but back then I didn't understand why.

Coach Bob was essentially succession planning for future years, and if the scrimmage went well, then he knew the program was in good shape. Starting with a 6-3 season in 1983 the Mariners put together 33 consecutive winning seasons and Coach Bob was head coach for 18 of those years. I would get frustrated when opposing coaches would say, "You guys just get good talent."

Yes, in a few of those years we were blessed with great talent, but for most of those years succession planning and a veteran coaching staff that stayed together created a system that created wins, not just talent.

So, in 2013 when we realized we had no kicker ready to be inserted into our lineup we had a decision to make. We watched Olivia kick for the JV and as the year went on, the JV head coach, Fregetto, gained confidence in Olivia and gave her several opportunities. No female had ever been a part of Marine City football and when Coach Fregetto asked what he should do with Olivia, I responded, "Use your best judgement and keep her safe."

Olivia recalled, "I approached the JV coach and told him I wanted to be his kicker. He wasn't sure at first and tested me at a couple of practices. He finally agreed, and I was officially a part of the football team. I don't think he knew quite what to do with me. Coach had me take part in tackling drills paired up against the smallest guy, bear crawling through the mud and had me play scout defense after he explained to me what exactly that was. I like to think I really earned my spot on the team by doing all of this."

What I remember most about watching Olivia during her JV year, was the absence of fear. Nothing in her body language hinted at fear, nothing in her approach hinted at fear, and when I asked her early in 2013 if she would be interested in kicking for us it was without hesitation an immediate, "Yes."

I told Olivia that everything on varsity would be 10 times faster than the JV game and that she would have to increase her speed when approaching the ball. She assured me she would practice with her dad and brother during the summer to meet the challenge.

Olivia's brother, Tyler, was our kicker in 2009 and Olivia's dad, Chris, was our soccer coach so I knew the best thing I could do was to stay out of the way and let them do the coaching.

"I wanted to step up to the plate, so my dad and I practiced kicking multiple times a week during the summer of 2013. Together we perfected my steps and timing, and increased both my distance and accuracy," Olivia recollects.

During practice, the word, FIRE, takes on a new meaning. If this word is ever yelled during practice, it means that the

Mariners must assemble the field goal/extra point team on the ball and kick it through the uprights before time expires. It can happen at any time during practice, and it simulates some late game heroics where we need a field goal to win as time expires. The first time we ran a FIRE DRILL in practice was when I knew Olivia would be our kicker. Fire...15,14,13,12. The field goal team raced onto the field and as the countdown neared zero, Olivia blasted the football through the uprights. No fear, no hesitation, no problem, Olivia was now our kicker, and we would embrace that.

One thing I most respected from Olivia in August 2013 was the way she spoke to our holder, Jarrett Mathison. "Jarrett, you got to get the ball on the tee quicker and angle the ball back slightly," Olivia would say with a firm voice.

I made it perfectly clear to the team that if anyone messed with Olivia or treated her badly, hellfire would rain down on them. Jarrett would simply take the feedback from this young lady and look at me and smile and shake his head. I would be a smart ass sometimes and say, "Yeah Jarrett, do your job," holding back a smile and a laugh.

Olivia's first game was probably her toughest...

"I remember my first varsity game like it was yesterday. We were away against Richmond, and I was so nervous. There were so many people in the stands, and I knew people were already talking about how there was a girl on the football team. They were doubtful to say the least. I felt an immense amount of pressure to do well—not only for my teammates but also to prove to all the fans that I was capable of being

Marine City's extra point and field goal kicker. We won the game, and I was 6/6 in extra points."

I remember a dad approaching me after the Richmond game, disappointed in his son's playing time and said, "Hell, even Olivia played more than my boy!"

My response was quick and simple, "Can he kick better than Olivia?" The father did not respond, and that abruptly ended our conversation.

I am proud to say that the players on the field goal/extra point team took great pride in protecting Olivia, but the game is unpredictable and sometimes things happen. When asked about this issue, Olivia summoned this response,

> "We were playing East Detroit, and I went out on the field to kick another extra point. However, this one didn't have a particularly good snap, and my holder, Jarrett Mathison, hesitated between getting the ball set for me and going for a two-point conversion. He was supposed to yell, 'Breakout' if he was going to go for two, and that was my cue to get the heck out of there. But because of the hesitation, I got caught in the middle of everyone, and I got tackled by an opposing player trying to get to the ball. While trying to stand up, another player hit my helmet and caused me to fall again, leaving me rattled. I got out of there as quickly as I could and sprinted to the sideline only to hear, 'Welcome to Mariner football,' from Coach Glodich. A teammate stepped on my calf causing a bruise that lasted for weeks, but my level of respect for them increased tremendously."

Having a daughter, myself, I knew that Olivia's parents, Chris and Mary, were putting tremendous faith in our coaching staff to keep her safe. She was instructed that if, "Breakout!"

was ever yelled during the point after attempt, she was to sprint to the sideline. In theory this was a good idea, but to see it in action on film was comical. We were not used to someone running away from the ball and Olivia took our instructions to heart and would sprint to the sideline almost as if a grenade were about to go off.

I will share more about Olivia in the next couple chapters, but I must point out that she set a school record in 2013 for the most extra points made in one season at 61. Even more amazing was that Olivia missed no extra-point kicks that year. The stat books say we were 61 for 65 in extra points that year, but the four misses were results of bad snaps and Olivia never got to kick the ball. She was perfect for the entire season, in her first varsity season.

Olivia's story is a book that speaks about...

Taking on new challenges to grow in life.

Attacking your fears head on and using massive amounts of imagery and repetition to create confidence.

Being a part of something bigger than yourself, and the joy you can receive from a team's accomplishment.

Courage and how courage can take on many shapes and sizes.

How anything can be achieved if you have the "fire" in your eyes.

Wait! did someone say, "Fire," 15, 14, 13, 12...

22

HOW COULD YOU?

THE OFFICIALS WALKED across the field and went directly to Daryn Letson. As a science teacher I have theorized why people are drawn to my good friend, Daryn. If we go scouting or we are out with the wives, it never fails that people will come up to Daryn and try to start a conversation. Daryn is not looking for their company and has no desire to start a conversation, but he is always cordial with them. My theory, which is well rooted in Newtonian Physics, is that his head is so extremely large that it has its own gravitational field. When I became head coach one of my first purchases was visors for the coaching staff. The visors had the one size fits all Velcro adjustable straps in the back. Daryn couldn't wear these visors even if the strap were adjusted to its max size. When he tried to put the visor on it looked like a thimble on top of his head.

The officials asked, "Are you the head coach?"

161

Daryn replied, "No sir, he is over there. He's the guy dressed like Rocky Balboa."

Saturday November 23, 2013, was the Mariners semi-final game played at a neutral site—Ortonville Brandon. The temperature on that day was 27 degrees with wind gusts ranging from 18 to 29 miles per hour. The day produced a bit of snow and some freezing rain, and when we reached the field, it was frosted over with snow. In my entire coaching career, I have never experienced a nastier day for a game. My goal that day was to not let the weather get into my mindset, so I dressed appropriately. Years earlier we had purchased light grey Nike® sweatsuits and, on this Saturday, I wore the sweatpants as my outer layer. I didn't care what they looked like, I cared that they would keep me warm. My wife, however, apparently did care and later asked me, "How could you wear those sweatpants on game day? They are so saggy in the rear it looks like you have a diaper on. Oh, my God, I was so embarrassed!"

Lansing Sexton was 12-0 and was considered by many in the newspaper world to be the best football team ever to come out of Lansing. They were loaded with talent, size, and speed and had a future NFL player on their roster. Rayshawn Wilborn, who now plays for the Denver Broncos, was a wide receiver/linebacker, and he was built the part at 6-4 and 220 pounds. Sexton also had a trio of running backs with their top back headed to Ferris State University in Avonte Bell. At 6-0 and 230 pounds, Avonte could literally run over people when he had a head of steam. This Saturday, the weather would test the capabilities of any offense, and the team that could produce first downs through their run game would have a huge advantage. We say it all the time to the kids, but this Saturday was truly *Mariner weather*, and we hoped to dominate the day with our WING-T-OFFENSE.

Marine City won the coin toss this Saturday. We kicked off and received the ball to start the second half. Midway through the 2013 season the coaching staff was not happy with our kickoff coverage, so we tried a little sports psychology. We told the kids that great kickoff teams were fearless, and we wanted the craziest, most fearless players on this unit, and we would nickname this unit as the Crazy Mother F***ers (aka CMF's). If they were placed on this team, then the coaching staff believed they were one of the most fearless players on our team, and we needed those players to start each game with a bang. We tried to place an honor badge on anyone who was placed on this team, and this was the Saturday that unit was tested.

Sophomore, Jacob Rhein, was our kickoff guy but was struggling with a meniscus tear in his knee. He was scheduled to have surgery after the season and each kick produced pain he had to deal with. He kicked off to start the game and pounded the ball to the 10-yard line. One of our main concerns during this game was the speed of Lansing Sexton and on this kick return the ball carrier quickly got to top speed as he headed right through the middle of our coverage unit. As he neared midfield, it looked like he had an opening to score but flying in from the side was one of our best CMF's, John Badger. John was a junior and as a wiry 5-11, 147 pounder, he was the epitome of a TEAM PLAYER. If you needed a running back for scout offense, he would volunteer; if you needed equipment put away at the end of practice, he would volunteer. John took pride in his role on the kickoff team, and it was obvious from the number of tackles he had in this role. John Badger prevented a touchdown on the opening kickoff and his pride in his role on the CMF team is a hint of the championship mentality needed for great teams.

Sexton started the opening drive near midfield and on their first play they completed a deep ball down our sideline. With heavy winds and snow falling, the passing game would be challenged on this day, but not on this play. Sexton had the ball now on the 19-yard line and was threatening to score. Three straight run plays followed, and the Mariner defense bottled up Sexton each time. On their fourth-down play, Sexton's quarterback rolled to his right looking for their big receiver,
6-4 Rayshawn Wilborn, and as the ball was thrown, our safety, Joe Mazure, stepped in front for an interception in the end zone.

Joe was part of a group of players in which I saw huge improvement, continuously, week-to-week during this playoff run. Sophomores: Dennis Fitzsimmons and Jacob Headlee, juniors: Kenton Rivard, and Griffin Lictawa, and seniors: Jake Shermetaro and Tate Sapienza also made huge improvements during this same time.

Marine City took over on their own 20-yard line and on the first play, Coach Letson utilized our T-FORMATION and multi-fakes and Tate Sapienza raced off left tackle for a 13-yard gain. Two plays later Tate again ripped off another 20-yard gain with the same play. After a nice completion to Jarrett Mathison out of the backfield, we stalled on this drive around the 10-yard line. We were disappointed that we didn't produce points on this push but realized that Sexton was committed to taking away Jarrett's run game, which would produce opportunities in other areas for our offense.

We forced Sexton into a 3-and-out and their punt landed near midfield. Handling punts with the wind and snow would be a challenge so we instructed Pete Patsalis and Jarrett Mathison to just let the punt bounce off the turf. On third-down we threw the ball to Pete in the right flats, and he appeared to have some running room. With a collision resembling a train wreck, NFL bound Rayshawn Wilborn closed the gap quickly and laid a hit on Pete from which most players would not get up. A huge moan from the crowd followed as Pete flew several yards in the air after the collision. Pete immediately bounced up and raced back to our huddle. Only in our huddle surrounded by his teammates did Pete finally show body language that he was in terrible pain. He fought his way through the pain and remained in the game, which of course cemented his WARRIOR CHARACTER to the coaches and his teammates.

The first quarter ended scoreless, and the conditions of the day affected the offensive plays of both teams. Midway through the second quarter we mounted a drive coming out of our own red zone. On second-down we ran Jarrett on a 34-power, and he broke a few tackles for a small gain. Well after the play ended, big 6-4 right tackle, Paul Carbone, came flying in and dove into the pile of players—looking much like Jimmy Superfly Snuka jumping off the top ropes during a WWF wrestling match! The officials threw a flag for a 15-yard unnecessary roughness penalty, and I immediately pulled Paul out of the game. I was too preoccupied helping Coach Letson figure out what to call on the ensuing second and 25 play to yell at Paul. The rest of the coaching staff lined up quickly, shoulder to shoulder with jaws clenched, as Paul neared the sideline.

One by one, each coach laid into Paul about his stupidity and Paul simply looked them in the eye and moved on to the next coach. It reminded me of the scene in the movie, *Airplane*, where passengers line up to slap a woman who had lost her composure, but our coaches never touched Paul. Memories like that amaze me as everyone on that team remembers that interaction but would have trouble remembering other details of the game. Paul's interpretation of the event makes me laugh every time he tells the story. "Oh man they let me have it, spit was flying and there was nothing I could say; I knew I screwed up."

The penalty killed the drive, and we were forced to punt—again scoring no points. Sexton capitalized on the next drive and scored on a 40-yard pass play coming off a toss play action. Sexton converted the extra point and led 7-0 with 6:26 to go until halftime. We failed to move the ball again and punted the ball back to Sexton where they started the drive on their own 17-yard line. Sexton gambled on their first down and took a shot deep down our sideline, but Joe Mazure was in perfect position to defend. Joe tipped the ball at the high point, and it deflected right to Pete Patsalis at midfield and Pete immediately changed direction and headed toward our end zone. Pete gained 25 yards on the return and put us in great field position as the second quarter was about to end. The Mariners put together a seven-play drive, mixing runs between Jarrett and Tate to score with just one minute to go till halftime. The wind disrupted the extra point snap, preventing Olivia from kicking and resulting in a failed attempt. The halftime score became 7-6 Sexton.

This was one of the rare halftimes where we took the team back into the locker room as the temperatures continued to fall. Our marching band had traveled to the game and was scheduled to play at halftime. They could not perform because many instruments were frozen and would not produce sound. I greatly respect our band director, David Uhrig, as he motivated the kids to make humming sounds with their voices and replicated tunes to the best of their abilities with their voices. The noise they created, like in the Country Day game, was a definite factor and we benefitted from their energy. In my mind Mr. Uhrig is a football coach who works with the marching band; I can't say it too often, "He is a TRUE MARINER!"

On the opening drive of the second half the Mariners again were put into a third and long scenario because of some false start penalties. The ball was near midfield and during this drive we used some of our spread formations. On third and 18 yards to go, Coach Letson called a fullback trap out of a spread formation. That was the beauty of how our offense had evolved—since our lineman didn't care about the specific formation—they had the same blocking rules. We could force teams to deal with multi formations, without creating more rules for our offensive lineman. The defense was forced to adjust to formations quickly which allowed us to attack while they were adjusting. The fullback trap to Jarrett surprised Sexton when he picked up the first down with a 19-yard gain.

This was the play of the game!

We kept possession of the ball and Sexton's offense off the field. After a 20-yard gain by Tate Sapenzia utilizing our 47 OFF-TACKLE PLAY, the Mariners scored to regain the lead. Thanks to linemen Jake Rueter, Kenton Rivard, Kevin Fitzsimmons, Josh Albo, Ethan Cleve, Paul Carbone, and Griffin Lictawa, Tate finished the day with almost 200 yards rushing against a tough defensive front. Tate weighed a slight 145 pounds yet took the pounding all day long. Despite being thin, Tate had a well-defined muscular build because of his commitment to the weight room. He absorbed every hit and bounced up quickly each time. Sadly, our two-point conversion failed, and the scoreboard read, 12-7 Mariners with 7:36 left in the third quarter.

Olivia was forced to kick off as Jacob Rhein's knee was not cooperating. This seems like a small note but ask any coach how they feel about 10 players competing against eleven players and the truth will be revealed. We had a great deal of confidence that Olivia would put the ball where we needed it and that our CMF kick off team could handle the challenge. Remember, we had always asked Olivia to sprint off the field when she would kick, essentially removing our safety from the team. Olivia Viney kicked a perfect cross kick to their 25-yard line and Mister Reliable, John Badger, made another great SPECIAL TEAM tackle.

During the ensuing drive, Lansing Sexton let Avonte Bell go to work. He punished us with three consecutive run plays from his tailback position, where he started seven yards deep. Football is a game of momentum and at 230 pounds and a decent speed, Avonte Bell was a tough ball carrier to bring down. On first down, he again received the ball and quickly gained 10 yards where safety Joe Mazure met him. Joe attacked his shoulder and grabbed on with his long arms. While Avonte was dragging Joe, the ball was stripped out of Avonte's arm and Joe recovered. Turnovers are a huge component to playoff wins and this was Joe's second turnover recovery.

The Mariners put together a 12-PLAY DRIVE but failed to score. The importance of a 12-play drive at this point in the game was clock consumption. One key play during this drive was a fourth and one conversion where quarterback, Alex Merchant, audibled out of our called play, signaling a quarterback sneak. The sneak gained five yards and got us a first down, and the clock continued to count down.

Sexton took over on their own 26-yard line and mounted a short drive before punting. The Sexton drive was foiled by a great blitz from our sophomore linebacker, Jacob Headlee. The Mariners next drive resulted in nine plays before we were forced to punt again. Dana O'Rourke handled the punting duties all day in the miserable weather and did a great job. Yet another Sexton drive was spoiled by a LINEBACKER BLITZ, this time coming from sophomore, Dennis Fitzsimmons. Sexton's punt landed on the Mariner nine-yard line with just 4:42 left in the game. The field position game was tilting toward Sexton and if we didn't get out of our own red zone, Sexton would be in a great position to finish the game.

Marine City's 2013 offensive linemen as a group was the best in the school's history. The proof in the pudding was the way they finished off big games, and this semifinal game was no different. The Mariners put together a drive with runs of +8, +11, +8, +18, and moved the ball from the nine-yard line to near midfield. We faced a third-down and twelve scenario and had to make a decision. If we failed to convert, Sexton could attempt a punt block or receive the ball back with about two minutes to go. If we converted the third downplay, we could run the clock out because Sexton had no timeouts remaining. We were headed into a brutal wind, so we knew our punt would be minimized.

We took a time out to discuss our play call and rode the RISK/REWARD TRAIN to Ford Field. Coach Letson called 400 BROWN DROP BACK, 5-X-9. This was a play action pass where we inserted Joe Mazure at left tight end and moved Pete Patsalis to our right-wing position. Joe would run a seam route right down the middle and Pete would run a corner route to *our* sideline. As the ball was snapped, Alex Merchant locked onto Joe and made the throw right down the middle of the field. Sexton had the play covered as three defenders surrounded Joe. Alex had to throw the ball early and on a flat line because the wind would have altered any other throw. The low trajectory and perfect placement of the pass allowed Joe to make a great catch in traffic, but he was immediately hit by all three Sexton players. When the pile unfolded, Joe had the ball wrapped in his arms like a prized possession. The Mariners had their first down, Sexton was out of timeouts, and the Mariners took a knee on the next two snaps.

The game ended with the sun shining and the Mariners victorious 12-7 on a frozen field.

The sun seemed to take some of the chill off the field and we celebrated and addressed the team. I remember being emotional after the win, knowing this team was about to head to Ford Field for the third time in school's history. I was rightfully proud of a team that was deemed underdogs two weeks in a row and had proved the papers wrong. The Mariners defeated schools loaded with an abundance of talent. This team of gritty, hardworking, selfless players were on a mission and the next stop would be another talented team that was also the defending state champs. Grand Rapids South Christian was on the clock.

23

MY LINES, MY LINES.

YOU COULD HEAR her booming voice all the way down the hall. Her energy was amazing, and she always walked with a purpose as if she were on a mission. The phrase, *larger than life*, seemed written with her in mind. Yes, she was a bigger woman with broad shoulders, but even so, her presence was undeniable. If she was in the room, everyone knew it because she might hold you accountable. When she got to my classroom door, she would stop and check in on me. "My baby, Ronnie, how are you today? How are those beautiful little ones doing?" No one else in that school called me Ronnie but her, and I liked it. Most of my friends from high school had called me Ronnie, so it made our friendship feel like we had known each other for years.

She was Penelope Burmann, and she had been the math teacher and cheerleading coach at Marine City High School for 32 years, starting in 1971. I considered her one of the most influential mentors in my early years of teaching and coaching.

She made it crystal clear from the beginning she would take me under her wing. "I am gonna make sure no one messes with you, Ronnie; there are some good people in this school, and there are some smucks." She was a galvanizing force in our school as she connected with every teacher and every kid. She had an incredible knack of connecting with kids who were shy, quiet, or somewhat forgotten by the student body, and she would involve them in some school activity.

One of her shining moments was the creation of a spring fashion show every year. The show would be sponsored by a local tuxedo and dress shop and would give a glimpse of the current fashion trends. She would hand pick seniors who may not have had any shining moments during the year and talk them into being in the show. She also recruited talent from the school and convinced them to perform between runway walks. What resulted was a packed gym and an incredible show—all for a $5 donation to her cheerleading program. The attendance was so large she convinced the janitors to move the bleachers off the wall and position them facing the stage so it would appear like a true theater. She recruited Tony Scarcelli, Bob Staskiewicz, and me for security and to monitor entrances for those who tried to sneak in. The show always drew a diverse audience as people could make the walk from town to the high school, which is exactly what *Sweet Burm* wanted.

There were countless lessons I learned from Burm, either through our direct conversations or observations. She had two boys go through the school and I was fortunate enough to observe her parenting skills. Matt and Nathan were both excellent student/athletes, and each played offensive lineman for the Mariners, but what impressed me the most was their involvement in other aspects of the school. When our twins were born in 1994, Burm immediately went into parental mentoring mode.

When I took over varsity basketball in 2001, our relationship expanded even further. Long bus rides during away games created opportunities for Burm and I to have meaningful conversations and I was always amazed at her balance of listening skills and intelligence. She preached often, "Ronnie, make sure those twins are exposed to everything. Don't funnel them into just one arena, allow them to experience all discrete events and all different atmospheres." She was a huge advocate for the arts and her boys were involved in band, theatre, and choir. She was also a huge believer in inclusion and wanted her students to shine in as many activities as time would allow.

Burm walked the talk as every year she hosted staff parties that would draw a varied teaching staff to her house. I was part of a younger wave of teachers and Burm was just one of a united group of veteran teachers who had come to Marine City at roughly the same time. My admiration was sparked by that group of expert teachers! I know their professionalism and consistency helped to mold my teaching style. Tony Cavis, Patricia Biebuyck, Don Chamberlain, and Charles Homberg were influential to me as a young teacher and following their lead, I became a better educator So, long before I ever became head football coach at Marine City High School, great educators influenced a mindset that every activity/group/team in our school was as important as the other—that no one group should overshadow any other.

When I became head coach in 2012 the voice of Penny Burman was always in my head. She had retired, and I no longer had the privilege to see her daily, but all the long conversations remained...fresh in my memory bank. I wanted to make sure I was visible at as many school functions as time would allow. My kids had graduated and were off to college and this freed up time. My wife, Kathy, was a willing participant, so we attended as many play productions, choir, and band concerts, and fashion shows as we could. I realized quickly that excellence was running rampant at Marine City High School. Burt Van Dyke with choir, David Uhrig with band, and Jay McCollough with theater created a three-headed horse for the arts. In the summer months there was nothing I loved much more than listening to Mr. Uhrig bark out orders to his marching band from his 20-foot scaffolding overlooking the football field. He held his band to a high standard, and it showed in every performance. I remember during one pep assembly; Mr. Van Dyke's choir performed a version of *Don't Stop Believing* by Journey and I immediately got goose bumps on my arm. I later shared with Mr. Van Dyke that was my body and mind's way of recognizing excellence and how inspired I was by their performance.

And then there was Jay McCollough and the school's play productions...

Jay started at Marine City in 1999 and much like Sweet Burm, was gifted in his ability to connect with many students.

His deep commanding voice is one part motivational and one part calming. He is a deeply religious man, but does a wonderful job of preaching kindness, compassion, and growth to his students as a role model versus the use of heavy scripture. He sees the good in students and plays to their strengths and creates banter in his classroom that the kids just love. Jay took over our theatre program at Marine City High School and still holds that title at the time of this writing. When I became head coach, there were a few athletes he inspired to be part of his productions, but his play practice conflicted with football practice times. Jay and I agreed to be flexible so these students could experience both the play and football.

It didn't take long to realize that theater students put in as much time to prepare for their performance as did my football players! The commitment he expected from his students and the passion they possessed rivaled anything we did in football. Every play I attended strengthened my respect for the arts and for the leadership that Jay commanded. He was also one of the most positively vocal fans in the stands during our home games. I am proud to say that Jay and I became great friends and remain so today. In 2013, as we prepared for our playoff run, Jay approached me with an idea.

"Ron. I just love what you are doing with the program and if you agree, I would love to give a little motivational talk to the boys before the playoffs start. It will take just 10 minutes, I promise." I knew the players would look at this in a positive light because they loved Mr. McCollough, so we set a time and day for Jay to talk with the team.

---

*What transpired was not just a motivational
talk, but a visionary look into what it would
take for the Mariners to succeed.*

It was not a talk, it was a full-fledged Google slide presentation with video clips, inspirational quotes, and personal stories. We sat and listened and just minutes into his presentation the hair on my arms rose. Jay started off with a video clip from the movie, *Coach Carter,* where the coach asked a player to perform pushups and suicide sprints as a form of discipline to rejoin the team. When the player puts out a valiant effort but falls short, Coach Carter explains he can no longer be on the team. Then in the slides that followed up the clip...one by one each player volunteers to help with some pushups and sprints, saying, "You said we were a team, when one player struggles, we all struggle, when one player triumphs we all triumph."

And then Jay snuck it in, "And let us run with perseverance the race that is marked out for us, Hebrews 12:1." It fit perfectly into what we would experience in the playoffs and help create the mindset on any day:

---

*Team and perseverance can
conquer Talent.*

He talked about a father who would push his paraplegic son in a modified wheelchair during marathons. "There is just something that gets into me when I'm out there competing with Rick and I can't explain it and I'm able to go faster," was the message in the next slide.

Jay finished his presentation with his personal story of a goal to run a 5k race with his son, Logan, and how they have inspired each other to get up early in the morning to train. Jay became emotional when reflecting on how strong his son's influence had been on him. "I can honestly say that without my son, Logan, I would not continue to train; we are a team." When he finished the talk, Jay thanked the fellas for their attention and quickly exited the room.

A wave of emotion ran through me as Jay walked out of my classroom. I have never been shy about showing my emotions to the team but as I addressed them, I had to pause several times to regain my composure. This man obviously had spent hours preparing a presentation for a group of athletes he was not directly connected with. He poured out his heart, and he dispensed an effort for the good of the entire school and channeled it through the 2013 football team.

Our players were inspired and if they hadn't cemented the foundation TEAM OVER TALENT yet in their mind, Jay's speech started a flow of exponential energy into this mantra. Once I released the players and sent them toward the practice field, I knew I had to go thank him. I sprinted down to his classroom where he was already working with the students preparing for the next play production and I stood at his door. When he saw me, he stopped, and we both looked at each other...smiling. Still reeling with emotions, I could not bring words to my mouth, so I walked toward him and gave him the biggest bear hug I could muster. "Thank you," creaked out in my emotional voice and then turned and walked out to the practice field.

There are moments in any man's life so profound that you remember them forever, and your emotions stir every time you recall the experience. This connection with Jay is a moment that stands up in my library and if Penny Burman were still here, she would be in tears. Tears of joy, Sweet Burm, tears of joy.

MISSED CALL, UNCLE LEO.

THERE ARE A thousand distractions in any week during the football season and one thing we constantly preach to the kids is, "Don't drink the poison." When a team is on a winning streak, people tend to jump on the bandwagon and praise the team without truly understanding the *process* behind their success.

> *We emphasize the process over everything else, and that is simply: evaluate your prior game, find areas to improve, and establish a plan of attack.*

When the topic of *poison* comes up in a conversation, it is important for athletes to respond with, "Thank you for your support, but we need to focus on getting better this week and working on things."

Luckily, the Marine City 2013 State Championship appearance would be the third emergence in the school's history and the third one for our coaching staff. We had experienced distractions in the prior two games and had felt extremely comfortable knowing how to deal with the week's challenges—but 2013 threw me a little curve ball.

As was my normal routine, when practice ended Tuesday at East China Stadium, I jumped in my Durango and pulled out my cell phone. One missed call was from a Grand Rapids newspaper reporter requesting an over the phone interview. The tone of the message from this young lady caught me by surprise, and if I were younger and dumber, it would have enraged my short temper. "Coach Glodich this is Sara from the _____ Times, and I need you to call me immediately. I have a Wednesday deadline and need information and quotes from you. Please return this call tonight so I can complete this task."

There was only one *Coach Glodich* way to deal with this young lady, and that was to ignore her request. When she called the school the next day, our secretary put her through to my classroom, "Why didn't you return my call last night, Coach?" she immediately attacked.

"Well Sara, I have a game to prepare for and to be honest you are not at the top of my priority list, but I will gladly call you later tonight."

Scrolling through other missed calls, one jumped right out of the phone and started my mind racing. Missed call. Uncle

Leo. 4:58 p.m. Uncle Leo Gorski was my favorite uncle and was also my dad's best friend. I loved this man like another father and spent countless hours at the Gorski house because his son, my cousin Mark, was also my best friend. Uncle Leo and my dad grew up in Detroit less than a mile from each other but did not become friends until they were drafted into the Army for the Korean War. The similarity of the last names put them in a group sent to the Fort Leonard Wood training camp in Missouri. "Hey Ron, this is Uncle Leo...I wanted to give you a heads up I took your dad to St. John's hospital on Dequindre this afternoon. He was really having a hard time breathing, and he asked me to drive him to the hospital."

On Sunday night, I had a phone conversation with my dad who mentioned he was battling a cold and a slight cough. I am sure he had been struggling on Sunday, but knowing my dad, I am sure he didn't want to be any kind of distraction during my championship week. My brother John was already at the hospital, and I managed to get in touch with him. "He has pneumonia Ronnie, and they want to give him a five-day treatment of antibiotics through an IV bag. They are going to keep him in intensive care until his oxygen levels increase."

My heart sank immediately. As a biology teacher I knew the danger of pneumonia for a man my dad's age. Ironically, the last time my dad had pneumonia was in the Army and it prevented him from going overseas during the Korean War. I asked my brother if I could use Tuesday night to prepare the rest of the week's practice plans and get Coach Letson and Coach Pollock up to speed if Dad took a turn for the worse, then I would join him at the hospital on Wednesday night. He agreed, and I drove straight home, shared the news with Kathy and got to work. What I experienced the next couple of days can best be described as a *playing sick* phenomenon.

I have experienced and have witnessed countless other athletes play some of their best games when they are sick. It seems as though the mind is forced to be so efficient when you are sick, that it has no room to wander. Although I was not sick, my mind was being forced into efficiency. As I planned for the week, some clarity shone through about how to attack the defense of Grand Rapids South Christian. I knew Coach Pollock and Coach Letson were the ultimate coordinators and was grateful when they volunteered to pick up some tasks to help clear my plate. When Wednesday rolled around, I spoke with a nurse attending to my dad and she shared that he was stable and not getting any worse, so I attended practice. I explained to the team my dad's situation and the possibility of me leaving practice.

The team's senior leadership from Pete Patsalis, Kevin Fitzsimmons, and Alec Adams had been amazing all year long. They established a crystal-clear business-like work ethic, and they understood the process we were preaching:

> FOOTBALL MENTALITY is where you have razor focus on the task at hand and you maximize every minute possible, so you are best prepared for each challenge.

> FOOTBALL MENTALITY also means you hold yourself accountable and demand the same from your teammates.

> FOOTBALL MENTALITY means you ignore distractions, minor injuries, and social distractions and win the upcoming game *during* your relentless preparation during the week.

*As coaches, we constantly preach to our
players that with proper preparation the
game is won on Tuesday and Wednesday.*

The captains, the seniors, and the major players on this 2013 team continued their excellence at each practice. My dad's health was a concern, but this team would allow nothing to knock them off the goals they established.

Visiting my dad in the hospital on Wednesday, I heard him use language I had never heard from him before. Brother John was already there, and Dad was explaining how uncomfortable the bed was and that he had not slept at all the night before. He was fatigued from the coughing and the pneumonia and had no appetite. His frustration seemed to peak when I walked into the room. "I don't want to stay here anymore, Ron. I can't get comfortable. Tell the doctor I want to go home."

I could tell my dad struggled even to share this with me and then his voice got louder, and he let it go, "I just want to sleep in my own f***ing bed!" I had never heard my dad use the "F" word before and it caught me off guard.

My brother John noticed the surprise on my face and the delay in my response and jumped in perfectly. "If you leave right now, the insurance company won't cover a penny of this stay. Is that what you want Dad, is that what you really want? I know you are hurting but you can make it through five days. You are certainly tough enough to make it through." John had never coached one day in his life, but I have told him countless times this was one of the best coaching speeches I have ever heard.

My dad immediately calmed down, and his voice quickly softened, "Ok, I will stay. I will stay."

Our Thanksgiving Thursday practice was scheduled for the morning so the players could have a normal Thanksgiving meal. Later that night I went to visit my dad again. John took the night off, knowing he would be with Dad Friday night during our game. When I walked into my dad's room, I noticed they had him in a chair, slumped over and lightly sleeping in this sitting position. Dad heard me walk into the room, picked his head up, and looked in my direction. There was a confused look on his face, but I ignored it and asked, "How are we doing today, Pop?"

Dad continued to look my way with an obvious confusion that quickly transitioned to anger, "Why are you climbing the walls, get down off those walls right now." I was stunned and stood silently. I had no clue how to respond to that statement. Luckily, my dad literally shook his head as if he were snapping out of a trance and said, "I'm sorry. I am seeing things. I am sorry."

"That's ok, Dad, let me go check with the nurse. Maybe some of the meds are messing with you. I'll be right back,"

The attending nurse explained that my dad had also developed sepsis, which is a blood infection, and perhaps some of his antibiotics may cause hallucinations. She warned that the sepsis was now their major health concern for him.

My head spun, and my emotions swelled. I did not want my dad to see me until I regained my composure, so I went into the stairwell and called my wife Kathy. "Hey, honey, I just saw Dad, and he is not doing so good, I think when the game is over tomorrow night, I might lose it emotionally and I just want to warn you." I could barely get out the last part of the sentence as my voice cracked.

Kathy paused and then her voice and calmness helped put me back on track. "They know what they're doing there, trust them. Keep a positive mindset and help to inject that into your dad. Everything will be all right."

Man, oh Man is she a rock, and she is so right!

I transitioned into coaching mode and walked back into my dad's room. "Ok, Pops, Nurse says that some of the antibiotics you are on may be causing some hallucinations, so this is somewhat normal. You must keep drinking fluids as much as you can, and you must start to eat. Have you eaten today?"

Dad seemed clear in thought as he answered, and we talked about the game. We discussed that hopefully he could watch the Mariners on TV and that the players were praying for him. As my visit extended, I felt more and more at ease and sensed the same from Dad. We all think of our dads as superheroes so to see them in any other state is an adjustment. But I know this: while my competitive spirit came from my mom, any toughness I had come to possess was genetically tied to my dad. He was a tough old Slovak—and believe it or not—never missed a day of work in his 39-year career at Michigan Bell.

I had faith he would pull through,
I had faith in the Mariners,
I had faith in God.

25

THROUGH A WALL.

IT WAS NOT my idea, but it was a great one. Periodically throughout the year I had asked individuals to come in and speak to the team about life after Mariner football. Most were former players, but on this occasion, we asked a former coach to speak to the team right before the game. Daryn Letson, my offensive coordinator, suggested that we bring Coach Bob Staskiewicz in to give the pre-game speech at Ford Field. "That is a fricking great idea, D-let. I will call him and ask," was my instant response.

Bob asked, "Do you want a rah-rah fire up speech or something more mellow?"

"I want them fired up about Mariner football, Bob. I want them to know how many people they represent."

"You got it, Ron, thanks for the honor," Bob answered.

Before we called on Coach Bob, we had several other influential people talk to the Mariners before a game. One such individual was Ralph Onesko who was a '97 graduate, a fierce competitor, and a guy who wasn't shy to share a little swag about himself. Ralph became a Major in the United States Air Force and before retiring, spent 24 years serving our country. During our district final game, he happened to be in town, so I asked him to speak to the team before kickoff. He shared with the men that the discipline and work ethic he developed during his days with Mariner football allowed him to succeed in the Air Force.

He reminded the Mariners that the words
spoken at the end of every practice,
"Discipline, self-respect, and victory,"
were a recipe for self-improvement and
continual growth.

And finally, he spoke how Mariner football had grown into a community in which hundreds of former Mariners eagerly followed the outcome of every game, some living in exceedingly difficult environments, and they got to escape for a short time during the *Friday night lights.*

Ralph was part of the 1996 team that defeated our stumbling block rival, the Marysville Vikings. That '96 team represented Mariner football may be better than any other team. Not one Division 1 player, not one massive specimen who would invoke fear into our opponents—no, just a bunch of undersized competitors who would fight to the bitter end.

During Ralph's moment in front of the team, I developed goosebumps,
gleaming with pride as I witnessed the transformation of a cocky scrapper we brought up as a sophomore
to a powerful presence
who commanded the room?

Another former Mariner we brought in was Kyle Zimmerman, who spoke to the team before the semifinal game against Lansing Sexton. He played with Ralph on the '96 team and played quarterback at Wayne State University. Kyle then taught and was the head coach at Pontiac Notre Dame Prep in 2013. We faced his team in our 2011 run to Ford Field, which was a competitive game that wasn't decided until late in the fourth quarter. When Kyle spoke to the Mariners, a cameraman from State Champs asked if he could film the pre-game speech. "I have no problem with that," was my response. A smile broke across my face, when not more than thirty seconds into Kyle's speech, the cameraman lowered his camera and walked out of the room.

Too many words starting with the letter "F" was the culprit that led to his exodus. "If you see something red standing, I want you to f___ hit it; if you see something red running, I want you to f_ hit it. I want these f___ to feel pain that only Mariner football can dish out," were Kyle's early words.

Kyle, like Ralph, was an incredible competitor and was also a gifted athlete. He became our starting quarterback as a sophomore and led his first team to the state semifinals in 1994. With a very disciplined work ethic, he was a key leader who helped bring about the mentality of COMPETE TO THE END in the 1996 team that allowed us to break through a wall of defeats from Marysville.

Kyle and I transitioned from coach/player to coach/coach peers, and I asked him to coach with me in the summer of 2013 for the Michigan High School Football Coaches All Star Game at Grand Valley State University. It was a great experience, and we roomed together which created some comical banter, as he did not appreciate my early morning routine nor my love of the band, Journey.

During the week of preparation for the 2013 State final game we also brought in the two brightest stars from our 2007 state champion team—John Lyszczyk and Brendon Kay.

John Lyszczyk was a 5-7, 150-pound cornerback on our defensive unit. He had the game of his life in the state finals and was a huge contributing factor in nullifying Country Day's star running back, Jonas Gray. Jonas was a legitimate Division 1 athlete who had a stellar career at Notre Dame and then played professionally for several years on teams like the New England Patriots, Miami Dolphins and finally the Tampa Bay Buccaneers. John had one highlight after another during that game—defeating lead blockers and tackling Jonas Gray for little or no gain. He played the entire game in attack mode and had laser focus like we had never seen before. He spoke to the team with that exact message, "Focus on your job, and block out all other variables because they don't matter. All your energy must be put toward your job; you must have the discipline to block out the big screen, to block out the band or the announcer, because they don't matter. Your job, and only your job, needs to be locked in your mind for the day."

John was a rare combination of great athleticism and great intelligence. I always considered him a smart cookie when he was in high school, but it made my heart swell to see him speak to the team with poise, make eye contact with every player, and speak with a pace that allowed our players to absorb his message.

Brendon Kay was the other member of the 2007 State championship team we were fortunate to have spoken to the team. Brendon was our quarterback that year and just one of three players in the last 40 years to play Division 1 football. In 2013 he was in his final season at the University of Cincinnati and having an off week, returned home. The day of state finals, he spoke to the team after our morning walk-through. He spoke to the team about:

Confidence and visualization.

Unity—and reminded them of the years they would sweat together toward a shared goal.

Self-worth—and how they must believe they belonged and how they deserved everything for which they had worked for.

Finally, he was very complimentary in speaking about the Mariner coaching staff and noted to the team that, *if the players continued to trust their game plan, and execute that plan, good things would follow.*

Brendon didn't have to do anything special to capture the Mariners' attention. His accomplishments during his days at MC were legendary and now he has created tons of success for himself and his teammates at Cinci. I have always said that what I love about Brendon Kay is his humbleness and his respect for those to whom he speaks. He was a perfect model of how we want our athletes to shake hands, maintain eye contact, and speak intelligently in any setting. Brendon always said, "Hello," to my dad and took the time to shake his hand. This meant the world to Dad, and his eyes would always sparkle when we talked about Brendon.

This mature behavior does not happen without great parenting and that is what Brendon experienced with his mom (Diane), dad (Chuck), and stepdad (Al). We were blessed to have Brendon come through our program. He was certainly a *once in a lifetime athlete*, but we were equally blessed to have parents who understood the big picture and constructed their child's humble persona. They were *once in a lifetime parents.*

Now, it was time to gather the Mariners off to the side of the main tunnel at Ford Field to listen to Coach Bob. They had created a makeshift locker room area with dividing curtains, dry erase boards, and chairs. I introduced Coach Bob to the team even though they all knew who he was. I quickly noticed that the players were not only locked into his speech, but nearly every one of our coaches like Daryn Letson, Matt Pollock, Andy Scheel, who had played for Coach Bob, were standing at attention (almost military fashion) at the back of the chairs. Coach Bob spoke of how he noticed right away when he took the job at Marine City, he would see little kids all over playing football in the yard, at the elementary school, or in the park. He knew he had walked into a community that loved football. He…

> Mentioned that during his head coaching days, no matter where he went in town he was always questioned, "How is this year's team going to be, Coach Bob?"

> Talked about loyalty to the program and how the coaching staff had stayed together for years.

> Shared conversations he had with me and Tony—assured that if we stayed together, we could bring home a state championship.

> Reflected on the players' loyalty to the program and how they played in junior football and were coached by high school players and that it was now their turn to coach junior football.

> Pointed out that Marine City was unique in this feature, where one group after another of Mariners have greatly influenced the next group of Mariners and how over time this created incredible passion for the team.

And finally, he mentioned how the passionate fan group had grown over the years and reminded them that the 2007

Marine City attendance at Ford Field may have been the largest in finals history.

The ending statement was a conclusion that it was time for this team to make their mark, to put up another banner on the walls of the high school gym.

"Now you get what you deserve!
You have worked your asses off to get to this
point. Have no regrets when you walk off
that field today."

He wished the team good luck, and the players reentered the tunnel that channeled them to the playing surface at Ford Field. You could feel the energy and focus that Coach Bob had ignited.

Matt Pollock emotionally declared, "Coach Bob fires me up like no one else, I would run through a wall for that man."

26

BLACK FRIDAY WITH FRIENDS.

BLESSED ARE THE people in this world who have one friend that makes them feel energized every time they see them. I am one of those blessed...and my lifelong best friend is my cousin, Mark. Whether it is a five-minute phone conversation or a week-long family vacation, when *Blood* and I get together it is like a dose of good medicine. Mark (Uncle Leo's son) knew 100% of what was going on with my dad and was a reassuring player who helped me stay focused on the week's objective.

During our warmup routine down at Ford Field, I allowed myself to look up into the stands and take in the energy. Literally the first person in the sea of orange that I spotted was Mark. He was standing next to my Uncle Leo and looking right at me. I pointed at him, then patted my heart and got back to the task at hand.

Another blessed friendship developed over the years re-energized my coaching passion in my final few years. Coach

John Kretzschmar's first true interaction with me was during a preseason scrimmage with Lakeview. "You ever run out of bounds again and that will be the last time you touch the ball; do you understand me, Son?" I had just lambasted a young running back and as I turned and walked back into the huddle, I looked at Coach K and gave him a wink. Coach K became our strength and conditioning coach during the time his three sons went through the program. Max, Jack, and Scotty Kretzschmar were dominant players with whom I immediately felt connected—mostly because of the similarity in our family's dynamics. Coach K was a retired police officer whom I believed was a pillar of fitness. His demonstrations of abdominal power had the kids amazed in the weight room and it was his endurance during end-of-workout challenges that made them willing students. His intellectual conversations and his insight into behaviors made our chats more like therapy sessions, which I sometimes needed. Just like Jim Labuhn, Coach K was extremely generous and took many items off my crowded *to do* list. Those actions were appreciated, but his friendship was priceless.

"Fatigue makes cowards of us all." So said General George S. Patton and Vince Lombardi. Year-end feedback from our seniors over the years highlighted a theme that many of them felt fatigued during the playoffs. In 2013 we wanted to keep our legs fresh during the week, so we shortened practices. This may have been one reason for our post season strength, but I believe the accurate explanation for our energy existed in lifelong friendships. Our senior class was such a tight-knit group that each in turn energized the other, which became contagious. Time and time again, during 6:00 a.m. Dawn Patrol in the chilly dawn of February, I would witness a groggy player walking in and then just seconds later find him laughing and joking with his group of friends. I saw the same thing as kids strolled into the gym at 9:00 a.m. on Friday, November 29, 2013, when we prepared to play our fifth and final playoff game. It was our morning walk-through and the final opportunity to cover the week's adjustments for Grand Rapids South Christian. It was Black Friday for most of Michigan, but it was Black Friday for the Mariners for another reason.

Following our morning walk-through, the boys returned to the school around 3:30 p.m. for final meetings. As we exited the school to load the buses, the community and parental support was something right out of the classic basketball movie, *Hoosiers.* A tunnel of fans of all ages filled the space from the sidewalk to the buses. After loading into the buses, we were escorted by the Marine City police and fire department for a quick tour through downtown Marine City. Streaming out of the downtown bars and restaurants, more fans gave their well wishes with several showing face painting and colorful signs! As we headed out of town, we passed Kade's party store, which had a sign on the side of the building that read, "WE BELIEVE," and several fans outside the store held signs bearing the same message. As we turned onto 26-Mile the BP corner gas station was packed with cars filled with fans passionately screaming their support.

*It was a magical combination of
local community members and
lifelong football fans...
forgetting their differences for one day and
striving for the same result for our blessed
young students/athletes.*

Once we arrived at Ford Field, we were led through the side entrance down the long, sloping tunnel to our locker room. The kids dropped off their equipment and headed into the stands to watch the second half of the Division 6 game.

And so, it began…

The changes to our normal pre-game routine were enormous. The players would soon discover that compared to what was the norm during the year, everything would be different on this day. During a normal game, we as coaches dictated every move and kept a close watch on transition times. At Ford Field we were at the mercy of the game officials, TV time outs, and the prior game's timing.

We were told to prepare for anything from 15 to 30 minutes to warm up. As the head coach, I felt the most important thing I could do was to educate my team in all that was possible. I had learned through experience that teenagers don't like surprises when faced with stressful activities, so any lead-in I could provide would minimize the potential of that stress.

Once the Division 6 game ended, we dressed and gathered for Coach Bob's pre-game speech and then headed out of the tunnel for our pre-game warmups. The roar of the Mariner fans was immediate, and it was clear to see that once again the Marine City faithful and the sea of orange would completely outnumber the fan-base across the field. It was estimated on this day that the Mariner sideline housed nearly 15,000 fans, and local Ford Field staff have shared it was the biggest crowd for any championship weekend.

I thought our kids were extremely focused and business-like during the whole pre-game routine. Coach Dave Osterland shared the same message with our kids during every post season victory, "You've done nothing yet, so keep working, you've done nothing—yet!" It was a message that spoke to humility and work ethic and our kids listened and responded. They were focused and ready, and it was crystal clear in their eyes.

The Mariners won the toss and chose to kick off, and on the second play of the game, South Christian's Division 1 quarterback, Jon Wassink, hooked up with the top receiver, Eric Van Voorst. The play went 52 yards and South Christian was up 7-0 with less than a minute expired on the clock. South Christian was the 2012 defending state champ and came into the game as heavy favorite. The team averaged 31 points a game on offense, with a stingy defense that yielded just eight points a game. They were a quick strike offensive team and hammered that point home on their first drive.

We failed to answer the score but were able to see the defensive alignment that South Christian would employ during the game. South Christian started their second drive on their own 40-yard line and were able to cross midfield before they were forced to punt. Coaches Matt Pollock, Andy Scheel, Dave Frendt, and Dave Osterland put together a game plan based on movement. The Mariners were in constant motion as the quarterback scanned the field during pre-snap. The defensive backs and linebackers especially were never in the same place twice, which made it difficult for the South Christian offense to get a steady read. The Sailors returned the ball to the Mariners, and as I always tell our players, "A good defense allows the offense to be more daring."

On our next possession, Coach Letson created confusion for South Christian by utilizing several formations. From an UNBALANCED LINE, to SHOT GUN FORMATIONS, to the old 2-TIGHT FORMATION, every play reflected a distinct pattern. The Mariners moved the ball right down the field and as the first quarter was about to end, the Mariners faced a third and six scenario. One of Coach Letson's *go-to plays* was called the BULLET, where the team sprints from the huddle to the line of scrimmage and tries to snap the ball as quickly as possible, leaving the defense with little time to adjust. On the first play of the second quarter, we did just that with a BULLET and (#47) Tate Sapienza cracked off seven yards and a first down. Three plays later saw Jarrett Mathison dive over Kenton Rivard who had bulldozed the Sailor defensive lineman for the score.

---

*Olivia Viney kicked the extra point and
became the first woman
in Michigan high school final history
to score a point in a game!*

Olivia shared her memory, "I didn't get my hopes up about going to Ford Field for the state championship until we had won the semifinals. Then it all became real. I had adjusted to the enormous crowds and the energy of our Friday night games, but this was going to be something entirely new. A huge, televised event with thousands of people watching the only girl on the field, and the first girl to play in a high school state championship football game."

"The pressure was enormous, but I was confident in myself. I hadn't missed a single extra point all year, and I wasn't about to mess up that statistic on the biggest stage of them all. Coach Glodich cautioned me the day before the game that the uprights at Ford Field are narrower, so I wouldn't be surprised when I saw them the next day. 'The width doesn't matter if you kick it in the middle,' he told me, and he was right."

The Sailors moved the ball deep into Mariner territory on their next drive, but quarterback pressures applied by our dynamic sophomore pair of Dennis Fitzsimmons and Jacob Headlee led to an interception. Jarrett Mathison picked off the overthrow and returned the ball 51 yards and back into Sailor territory. With a serpentine action, Jarrett wove through the field displaying his speed and agility and the Mariner fans and the sideline exploded with excitement.

During the game I was not able to hear crowd noise. My focus and double-eared headphones blocked out nearly everything but watching the TV broadcast years later was magical. The increasing roar of the crowd as Jarrett dodged tacklers caused my heart to pound and my blood pressure to spike as I relived the moment. Coach Letson dialed up a nice play action pass on first down and Alex Merchant found a wide-open Pete Patsalis for a 40-yard touchdown pass. Olivia converted, and the Mariners were on top 14-7 with 7:12 left until halftime.

South Christian, in true champion form, quickly answered our score. On the fourth play of the next drive, quarterback, Jon Wassink. ran off right tackle and raced 50 yards for the score. The extra point was good, and the score was tied 14-14 with 5:36 till halftime.

The Mariners answered this challenge with another score of their own. Tate Sapienza turned a sharp corner going to his left and outraced the Sailor defense for a 20-yard score. With another Olivia extra point, the score was now 21-14 with just 2:05 till halftime.

Starting the next drive on their 35-yard line, the Sailors went into a two-minute offense with their highly recruited quarterback. With just 37 seconds left in the half, the Sailors were forced into a fourth and 10 situation. Quarterback, Jon Wassink, found a receiver crossing the middle of the field and picked up 27 yards for the first down. Undersized but aggressive, our cornerback, Tanner Star, when attempting to put on the brakes and change direction, injured his knee and was out for the balance of the game. During the same play, Jarrett Mathison was blocked with a helmet-to-helmet contact the officials did not call.

Three plays later, the Sailors scored with just 12 seconds left in the half. The score going into the locker room would be 21-21 and the Mariners would be without Tanner Star in the second half and help from Jarrett Mathison was questionable.

The game started to take on the resemblance of a heavy weight boxing championship.

Each team landed punches, showed weaknesses and strengths, and had their conditioning and toughness tested. The Mariner coaching staff assembled in the Ford Field tunnel, and we all agreed that we were exactly where we wanted to be. We had proven to be a tenacious team in the second half of every playoff game so far in the season, and knowing the contagious influence of the senior class, we felt we could close it out if we scored first in the third quarter. *Twenty-four minutes to history* had long been the theme during our halftime adjustments.

"The 2013 Marine City team played like it had a serious chip on its shoulder, and justifiably so. I think a lot of people doubted that team from Game 1 through Game 14 because the year before, the conference they played in showed a real lack of "star" power. And sure, unlike the previous two teams that had made the Finals, they didn't have a Division I kid leading the charge. But kids like Pete Patsalis, Jarrett Mathison, the Headlees, the Fitzsimmons kids, etc.—those were incredible high school football players, and they were the perfect kids for that team at that time. I think they knew how good they were collectively, and they were determined to prove everyone wrong. It started with the Week 1 win against Richmond, and I think losing to St. Clair—a ridiculously good St. Clair team, mind you—in Week 8 probably only fueled that fire more."

I am honored to include that quote from one of my favorite reporters of all time, Paul Constanzo, of the *Port Huron Times Herald.*

27

Welcome to My World, Son.

THE HOODIES WERE pulled over their heads and their eyes looked straight down at their feet as they walked. It was a painfully slow walk that would resemble a horror movie as though they were zombies walking through a cemetery. They eventually met at the practice garage and awaited orders. It was 8:30 a.m. this Saturday morning in Marine City and the varsity players were assembling for a day of Junior Football. In contrast to the lethargic varsity Mariners, would be energetic fourth and fifth graders who would shoot out of their cars like they were headed to Disney World. A couple of the braver pints would mess with the older players, knowing they were in no mood to take chase. I would welcome the boys in the garage with some fresh donuts from Paul's Bakery, and some life would come back to their body. My favorite phenomenon: "Coach, these kids don't listen, they are crazy," a player would comment.

207

My response with a big smile on my face, "Welcome to my world, Son!"

In 2002 Marine City Junior Football was established as a non-profit organization with its own State ID number. Tony Scarcelli was the founder and an amazing coach with whom I had the privilege to work nearly my entire career. His coaching record in the seven years as head coach will most likely never be replicated—80 wins to just eight losses. He averaged 11 wins a year and just one loss in his tenure, a 91% winning percentage, but his greatest contribution could be the formation of our junior football program. St. Clair had started a similar program in 2001 and with help from St. Clair's, Brian Mahaffy, Tony created a Marine City version of their junior football.

Tony created a Board of Directors, and we discussed what we wanted the program to look like and how it should be run. One pillar of the program would be that the younger kids in the program would be coached by current varsity players. Tony's logic was simple, and it might be one of the greatest contributors to Marine City Varsity football's sustained success over the years. By having the current varsity players coach, we could control what was being taught to the younger players. By having them coach, we could also force our varsity players to a whole new level of knowledge and understanding of our systems. And finally, by having our players coach, we could minimize the *win at all costs* parental mentality sure to reveal its nasty head as we emphasized both skill development and fun. The format was simple, two practices a week, usually following the Monday and Wednesday varsity practices. Fast-moving practices are only 90 minutes long, followed by a game on Saturdays. The last week of junior football games would be played on the turf of East China stadium, a tremendous thrill for the younger players.

I can remember a frustrated dad pulling me over during one Saturday game, "Coach G, my son Bobby has not run the ball all year," the dad complained.

I responded, "Well, Mr. Jones, we have asked Bobby several times if he wants to try running the ball and he has shared he is not ready. When he is ready, we will give him a try. Right now, he is enjoying himself and to me that is the most important thing."

The junior players would be wide eyed when their Friday night heroes were there to give them instruction and coaching. Their attendance at our varsity home games became common and they could see some of the same plays they were being taught in action on the stadium turf. It was the reinforcement of a system that would remain intact to this day. Tony had the help of a longtime assistant, Jason Bell. Jay also coached with Joe Fregetto on the JV and would be a constant in our press box on game day...having the thankless job of setting up the headphones. When Tony transitioned out of the junior football lead, Gary Griffin worked with Jay Bell for several years and created growth in the program by adding fourth and fifth-grade levels. Gary also coached our eighth grade for years and had his kids running an advanced offense. Coach Griffin was also on the headphones for us during game day, and always did a solid job, but during the state championship it became evident just how enormous. his contribution was.

The weaving together of youth and varsity players also created a connection years later that was still intact when some of the junior football players became varsity players. The former Mariners would joke with me, "Coach G, he learned that from me during junior football."

My response was a soft, genuine, "No doubt, Brother, no doubt."

There have been a few parents who have advocated for Marine City to join the Thumb Area Football League (TAFL), which is run and coached by dads. Local teams travel from town to town on Saturdays and play against rival towns. I suspect this could succeed if you had the right dads running the program, but I would not change our model...because it continues to reinforce our system.

We commonly face teams with more talent...especially when we make deep runs in the playoffs. Our system has allowed Marine City football to have consecutive playoff appearances and consecutive winning seasons for which most schools would kill. The way we double team...the way we carry out fakes...the way we swarm to the ball on defense...is something engrained in our young Mariners. The 2007 Mariners as state champs were the first group of junior football players to come up through the ranks. Everyone knew about Brendon Kay at an early age, but I specifically remember seeing Johnny Lyszczyk in a junior game and saying, "That kid is a player."

The 2011 team was the first fourth and fifth-grade group to go all the way through our program. The Kroll brothers and Anthony Scarcelli dominated the junior games, and it was clear they would be major contributors. And now— with the help of our junior football program—the 2013 team continued the run of success. Many of the players' tight=knit friendships started on the junior football practice fields, and when years of sweat and hard work create bonds, they become difficult to break or loosen. The 2013 players had been faced with myriad challenges over the years, and now with just one half a football career remaining, they faced their greatest test. It became crystal clear at halftime in Ford Field what their intentions were for the second half.

28

SADDLE UP, BOYS.

As THE HALF ended, I made a bee line toward the head official. I was not happy about the helmet-to-helmet collision not called on Jarrett on South Christians' last drive. "There was helmet-to-helmet contact on that last drive and you guys missed it. That can't happen in a big game like this," I shared my frustrations.

"Coach, we will keep an eye on it moving forward, but you have to help me with your offensive linemen," he quickly answered. "They keep singing that Sports Center jingle every time you guys have a big play; technically we can flag you for taunting," the lead official noted.

"I will talk to them," I growled back in frustration.

As I walked into the Ford Field tunnel, my mind was scrambling trying to decipher the official's last statement. "Sports center jingle, sports center jingle, what the hell is he talking about?" When I met with the team, we immediately broke into offensive and defensive groups, and as was our normal procedure the offensive lineman sat in formation in the front of the group. "The lead official is telling me you guys are singing some sort of jingle," my voice tapered off and reflected my confusion.

"Coach, we sing the Sports Center jingle, *da na ump, da na ump* as if it was a *top-10 play*. We do it to piss off their D-lineman," Kenton Rivard shared with a big smile on his face.

"I respect that...but knock that shit off. We don't need a taunting penalty in the second half," was my stern response.

A good offensive line can be the most powerful weapon on a high school football team, and that is what we had in 2013. The ability to put together long drives and eat up clock to keep opposing offenses off the field. In our playoff run we consistently wore teams down and owned the fourth quarter with our ball control offense. I received great feedback from the linemen at halftime-especially from Paul Carbone. As goofy as that big lug was, he always saw the game clearly and always gave great feedback for changes we might need to make. Our offensive line had swagger to them and rightfully so because they knew their strength was an enormous advantage. They also held each other accountable, and the offensive huddle would often become testy when they challenged each other. We rode the offensive line horses all year long and that would not change in the last 24 minutes of the season. My message as we headed out for the second half was, "Saddle up, boys. Let's finish this thing—like we have done all year long—we own the fourth quarter!"

The Starburst kickoff return provided the spark we needed to start the second half of football. South Christian in their previous kicks had done a good job of kicking the ball into the corner, but on the opening kick of the second half their kicker shot the ball right down the center of the field. Jarrett Mathison took the kick and immediately turned his back to the defense. In rapid succession, Tate Sapienza, Pete Patsalis, and Trevor Quandt converged on Jarrett and took their fakes wide to the sideline. Jarrett kept the ball and wove his way through the crisscross of blocks being executed. Ethan Cleve took out a Sailor defender right before he got to the ball and Jarrett continued untouched until he got near midfield, where things heated up.

A South Christian defender got a hold on Jarrett's sleeve and spun him around—Jarrett maintained his balance and spun out to his right where Trevor Quandt laid the final block that sprung Jarrett to the end zone. The end zone camera caught all the action, and the return was a beautiful thing to watch. The footage of the return went viral and was even discussed on one of ESPN's talk shows. In the end zone, Jarrett hugged his teammates and went into his familiar head nod routine. He was leading by example and saying with his body language, "They can't stop us boys, they can't stop us."

South Christian once again answered with a long 12-play drive that ended with a one-yard quarterback-sneak. With the extra point conversion, the scoreboard read 28-28 with 6:04 remaining in the third quarter. The Sailors next kickoff was a short cross-kick that gave us decent field position and we tried a fullback trap on our first play, which was stuffed for no gain.

Coach Letson and I have always meshed well with our play calling philosophies and I told D-let, "I want to try something. I sense some fatigue overtaking South Christian, so I think that if we could score quickly again that their spirit might falter." He agreed and I quickly called a play we had just inserted for the championship game that would attack a three-deep coverage.

In a double tight formation, we put Pete Patsalis in motion to his left and ran some sweep play action. Joe Mazure ran a post pattern right at the safety and Jarrett ran a wheel route out wide to our sideline. It was a unique combination that allowed Pete to run right down the hash uncovered and with perfect protection quarterback, Alex Merchant, delivered a strike. Pete went 64 yards and caught the ball in stride for the touchdown. Olivia converted, and the score was 35-28 with 5:11 remaining in the third quarter. I remember running over to Alex and giving him the biggest hug because his ball was so perfectly thrown. As I watched the replay, it was incredible to hear the roar of the crowd build as they saw a wide-open receiver, saw the catch, and then the race for the score. Pure adrenaline!

In South Christian's next possession an ALEC ADAMS SACK forced the Sailors into a fourth and long. On the punt return, Jarrett ran out of bounds on our sideline and got tied up with a Sailor defender. None of our kids talked smack to the lonely Sailor, but Coach Fregetto took the opportunity to lay some UP (upper peninsula) verbiage on the poor soul. Coach Fregetto is legendary and does an amazing job with our JV program. We would have none of our success without Joe's hard work year after year. He has the toughest job on our staff because he must constantly battle players being taken up to varsity and depleting his squad. To see him talk smack and have fun on our sideline was his due reward.

On our next possession we hit Joe Mazure on a tight end seam route for another big play. Later when faced with a fourth and one situation we ran our bullet play again and Tate Sapienza went 27 yards and was stopped just short of the goal line. On that play, Jarrett Mathison pancaked a Sailor defender, which cleared the path for Tate. The third quarter ended with a first and goal scenario on the one-yard line.

The Mariner sideline went into the fourth-quarter ritual of holding four fingers up to the sky—a tradition Coach Bob started as a way to emphasize finishing the game with your best effort. As with many of Coach Bob's traditions, it remains a main stay of Mariner football.

The call on the next play was a 43 wedge, and the offensive line created a push that enabled Jarrett to easily score. Olivia converted the extra point, which was her sixth on the day. Snapper, Josh Albo, ran to Olivia after the kick, and with face mask to face mask, he congratulated her. He knew she had just broken the school record for the most extra points in a season. Not only was Olivia the first female to score in a state championship game, but now was considered the most successful kicker in Mariner history. The camera focused on Olivia and her smile lit the humongous TV screen at Ford Field. I had preached all week to ignore the cameras and lock in on your opponent, but if there was one exception I would allow, it was for our Miss Olivia. The scoreboard read 42-28 with 11:54 remaining in the game.

South Christian would not go away and mounted another successful scoring drive. They scored quickly taking just four plays to go 65 yards and converted the extra point to make it 42-35 with 10:04 remaining in the fourth quarter. On the sideline Coach Letson and I gathered the offensive lineman and told them, "It's time for you to mount up, boys, and take over this game."

They accepted the challenge, and it was clear in their eyes they knew what had to happen. Eating seven minutes off the clock the offensive line bull dosed their way down the field and had the Mariners sitting in a third and seven situation on the 19-yard line. I called a timeout to get the right personnel into the game and we dialed up another play action pass. Alex Merchant found Pete Patsalis on the right sideline where Pete made a diving extension to get the ball to hit the orange pylon. The sideline official raised his hand upwards to signal touchdown and our sideline erupted. Olivia converted, and the Mariners led 49-35 with 3:45 left in the game.

South Christian went into two-minute offensive mode again, just as they had at the end of the first half where they scored quickly. This time, the defensive line led by Kyle Scharnweber and Scott Steinmetz, forced the quarterback out of the pocket...rolling to his right. With his Division 1 arm, the Sailor quarterback threw the ball 50 plus yards toward the end zone. Jarrett Mathison was in perfect position for the interception and caught the ball over his shoulder and immediately went to one knee in the end zone. We took over on the 20-yard line and it was settling in for all involved—this game was essentially over.

A wave of emotions entered as one coach after another came by to give me a hug. I held up just fine until Andy Scheel gave me a hug like only Andy can. Andy is a big man and his hug, and his long arms, consumed me. Andy was a former student, teacher aide, and player and we had been close for many years. He held on for a little longer than most and shared that he was proud of me. I couldn't help it as some water entered my bloodshot eyes. The truth was...

This week presented challenges, but our coaching staff remained focused, and I couldn't be prouder.

I couldn't be prouder of the kids and how they performed on the biggest stage possible.

The community and support during the playoff run made me incredibly proud.

The win was a program win, with each member of the coaching staff contributing to the entire success.

As the trophy presentation started, I searched out Jarrett to thank him for his willingness to put the team over individual status. I looked for Alex and congratulated him on a nearly perfect game as quarterback. And finally, I found my big horses and thanked them for the great ride. After all the celebrations and interviews were done, we headed back to the Ford Field tunnel, and one person stayed behind to walk with me.

Brendon Kay happened to be home from Cinci for the weekend and we had him on the sideline. He walked with me back through the length of the tunnel and reflected on both state championships. It was a special walk for me.

Marine City is a football town—they were ready to celebrate this victory, and we were about to discover just how crazy our fans can be.

29

Where's The Trophy?

STANDING OFF TO the side. Jim Labuhn met with an MHSSA official and received the white signature football that goes with the championship trophy. I am sure he knew the official somehow because he seemed to know everyone. They chatted for a short while before he moved on. The stadium announcer had just heralded us as the 2013 Division 4 State Champions and our four captains, (Pete Patsalis, Kevin Fitzsimmons, Alec Adams, and Kenton Rivard) walked to midfield to receive the trophy. The team followed, and they formed a huge huddle with hands raised and their index fingers extended.

He was Jim Labuhn, and he was our statistician for years, but that title does not do service to what he brought to the program. I consider Jim to be the most generous man in Mariner football history; a plaque outside the locker room at East China Stadium proclaims the same. His father was mayor of Marine City, where a bridge in town carries his father's name; somehow, football allowed the son to create his own legacy.

He did an amazing job of taking jobs, tasks, and myriad to do's off my list so I could focus on more football.

He did the same for Coach Bob and for Coach Scar and became a fixture on the Mariner sideline.

He was a firefighter for years before transitioning to fire investigations in the Mt. Clemens area. If the Mariners needed something done for the locker room, the weight room, or the practice garage, just one mention to "Buhner" and the job would get done.

He would take no money for expenses and would brush it off by saying, "Just get me next time, no worries."

Unfortunately, we lost Buhner to colon cancer in 2015 after 30-some years working with the program. Fortunately, his son, Jesse, has stepped in and picked up right where Jim left off, and we continue to benefit from the great generosity of the Labuhn family.

Laying on the ground, trophy centered in the huddle, the Mariners had their pictures taken and then made their way to the sideline where most of the fans had not moved. There was a group of players from the state runner-up team of 2011 wearing their orange jerseys and high-fiving many on the team. Aaron Loconsole, Anthony Albo, and Donny Upleger were some of the 2011 alumni who sat in the front row. Some of the Mariners climbed up the wall for an embrace with the fans which, of course, did not sit well with the Ford Field security, but they chose to stand back, knowing the fans had them outnumbered. Usually, teams scurried off the field with another game waiting in the wings, but this was the last game of the night, and the Mariners would enjoy this victory for as long as they could. Senior, Ben Jackson, ran over to the conductor stand where our marching band director, David Uhrig, proudly stood. Ben was involved in the marching band and had a great connection with Mr. Uhrig, so he climbed to the conductor stand and gave Mr. Uhrig an enormous hug— after which Mr. U directed Ben to conduct the Mariner fight song. Together, man and boy, they conducted the music and our wonderful marching band infused the fight song into the celebration.

Waiting outside Ford Field near the buses was my wife, Kathy, and our twins. It was very fitting that we took time to exchange long, emotional hugs. On the bus ride home, I was able to call my brother, John, to get an update on my dad. They could not watch the game live at the hospital and had to rely on twitter feeds for score updates. He said it was torturous waiting for updates, but it led to a glorious celebration. Dad was doing better and was scheduled to be released the next morning. I gladly volunteered to pick him up and take him home the next morning. This was an immense relief, and it allowed me to refocus on the celebration at hand.

I genuinely enjoyed bus rides home after a big win, but it had nothing to do with football. The 2013 team were fans of country music and always asked for a country station to be put on the radio. When a good song came on, the bus became a failed choir concert as the boys did their best to sing along.

There was something incredibly satisfying about hearing them all sing together—with pure joy in their untuned voices.

On this ride home we were escorted on I-94 by a Border Patrol officer who stayed with us until we reached the end of 26-Mile. My dad called 26-Mile the longest road in Michigan and on this night the 12-Mile, straight as an arrow road, went by like a flash. Once we neared the Ole Cheese House party store, we saw the lights of the cars. For nearly three miles, cars had parked on the side of 26-Mile with their lights on and horns blasting as the buses drove by. People were outside their cars, their faces gleaming in joy, waving their hands to support the Mariners. When we reached the end of the road and were about to make a right turn toward the high school, I noticed fireworks exploding on the north side of 26-Mile. This colorful scene as buses made their turn with fireworks going off in the backdrop, made each person involved feel like they were on a Hollywood movie set.

We bypassed the school and went directly to the main street in downtown Marine City, now being escorted by our local police. Police chief, Jim Heslip, was a former Mariner, a hell of a player, and was now also coaching with us. The street was packed, and people were standing in the streets...many of them with beverages in their hands. The boys rolled down the bus windows and took in the celebratory noise. People quickly converged on the buses wanting to slap hands and connect with the victors.

What really made my emotions run wild that night was to see the wide range of ages in the street. From the youngest fans in Marine City to the most mature and ageless—the faces all were smiling and celebrating with the boys, the band, and the cheerleaders. It was a moment in time that you wish you could bottle and drink from when needed. Luckily, our outstanding videographer, Scott Whiting, filmed much of it and included his footage in the year end highlight film.

I remember little of the conversation with the team at the high school, but I knew everyone was eager to meet up with loved ones to celebrate, so we kept it short. After the game, I went home and took my time getting cleaned up for the after party. Kathy also shared some of her experiences at the game. "I was so nervous during that game. How do you stay so calm?" she asked with a big smile. I always loved my wife's interpretation of the game because she sees the game so literally and sees things I would never notice. She celebrated with Gunnar and Gabbi after each score and shared how she felt joyous but exhausted at the end of the game.

We headed to the Riviera Restaurant where the after party was planned. Owned by Angelo and Mary Beth Patsalis (parents of captain, Pete Patsalis) they have always been most supportive and generous to the Mariner football program. As we entered the restaurant, the packed crowd paused, hushed, and gave Kathy and I a round of applause.

Again, a moment in time...like something out of a movie script and it melted our hearts.

We meandered to the booth area where most of the other coaches were sitting and getting after it. I hugged several parents on the short path and shook a bunch of hands. I have never been a big drinker, and I knew I was going to pick up Dad early in the morning, so I sat back and enjoyed watching our coaches celebrate. Coach Letson's sense of humor has always been one that just cracks me up, and he was busy telling stories of some of our bizarre exchanges on the headphones. "If people only knew what he says sometimes," D-let shared with the group.

On most nights, the bar would close at 2:00 a.m., but when your captain's dad owns the bar, that time might get extended. Kathy and I snuck out the side door of the restaurant around 3:00 a.m. because I knew D-let would not have let me escape easily. The next day, I asked D-let where the trophy was and he honestly said, "Ron I have no idea, I remember last seeing it around 5:00 a.m."

"Well, hopefully it shows up, and it's not for sale on the black market right now," was my somewhat flippant response.

30

THEY RAN INTO THE RIVER.

HIS YOUNG DAUGHTER, Nadia, just barely came up to his waistline. Her beautiful smile stretched ear to ear, and she wore a winter hat embellished with a skull and cross bones and pink ribbons on the front. His son, David, was to his left as they posed for pictures, and he was in his glory. David was a wide-eyed sponge who was a student of the game when most kids his age couldn't tie their shoes. The night sky behind them was pitch-black, except for a sprinkling of distant lights from the Canadian shoreline.

Andy was dripping wet and freezing, but still posing for pictures. His smile led you to believe he was enjoying the moment, but the trembling shoulders painted another picture for his body. Scott Whiting was interviewing him because—as promised—Coach Andy Scheel had just run into the frigid cold St. Clair River at the conclusion of the championship parade in downtown Marine City!

On this occasion, Kyle Scharnweber, Brandon Rhein, and Kevin Fitzsimmons joined Coach Scheel as they all posed for pictures. It was here the seed for this book was planted—I had turned to my wife Kathy and said, "This is amazing, it's like something out of a movie or a book, I can't believe the turnout."

On camera Scott asked Andy, "Did you really think you would be running into the river three times?" Andy had the perfect response, "I honestly really did. It is far and away the best football team I ever worked with, and I felt that way back in July. We needed to have some more fun, we were grinding, we put some expectations on ourselves, and I threw this out there as a silly thing. Those kids are great, our coaches are phenomenal, this community is incredible, and this is a community championship for sure."

The parade crowd had spilled over onto the beach, and it was literally packed. Standing shoulder to shoulder, the crowd formed a 20-yard tunnel from the lifeguard stand to the water. The only light provided was from the floodlight attached to Scott Whiting's camera. The boys joining Andy had their shirts off and were jumping up and down to stay warm.

At the end of the tunnel and glowing like cats' eyes in the night, was the board Andy had created during the season. It was being held over his head by Eddie Crampton. Andy's message was simple. The board had chain links and the word TEAM, and he preached how each chain link represented a player on the team and the chain's strength depended on the weakest link. As the word, TEAM brightly reflected in the low-level light of Scott's camera. I thought to myself, *how appropriate is that,* and then with no hesitation...Andy led the trek.

———❧———

They ran single file into the pitch-black water of the river and with the dark night sky you could barely see them until the water splashed around them as they popped out. The buzz from the crowd turned to a glorious roar as Andy and the players turned and faced the crowd with beaming smiles on their faces.

It was an amazing ending to an equally amazing parade that the community put on for us and came out in thousands to attend. The boys were on flat bed trailers and the coaches were in the back of some pickup trucks. The parade started at the south end in the Holy Cross parking lot and progressed north to the city beach. Much like the state championship night, the street was packed with fans of all ages.

> *The players and coaches were in a moment of time that many didn't realize was a once in a lifetime experience.*

This type of support, this type of community swell, is not the norm. As Coach Bob had told the kids in Ford Field, "Marine City is a special place, and the parade is just one more bullet of proof."

A RUN TO THE RIVER | Ron Glodich

31

THE BOYS OF WATER.

"**BE FRIENDLY BUT** be cautious with what you say. Find a parent or two that you trust and ask them for honest feedback and to keep their eyes and ears open for potential problems." These were the words and advice from Coach Bob when I took over the program. Craig Headlee was at the top of that list and actually gave me a big ole bear hug the moment he first saw me after the head coaching announcement. Craig and Sandy Headlee had four boys go through the program and each boy was eventually a captain for the Mariners. Over a 10-year run, the Headlee boys put the Mariner program on their back with their outstanding play. Craig was a starter on the 1986 state championship team in Marysville with Walt Braun at the helm, so he had seen good coaching in his day. Sandy became one of those *do it all* moms who helped with sideline pictures, senior night pictures, organizing team dinners, creating Halloween gift bags for the players and the list goes on and on. Craig was our district's IT director and provided critical help with camera rear shots, scoreboard maintenance, and film breakdown. At the end of each season, Craig would spend hours putting together a highlight film sneak peek that would be unveiled at our year-end banquet. The players loved his work each year, and it became the perfect ending to any season. The thing I respected the most about Mr. Headlee was his diplomatic way of letting me know when I screwed up in a couple of scenarios. Craig was also someone I highly trusted, and I appreciated his feedback, but the Headlee family's first significant contribution to Mariner football was their commitment to being Water Boys.

The Water Boy Legacy is potentially another book in itself as Coach Bob quickly established the guidelines for anyone who desired this position. Bob clarified that if any water boy wanted to be on the sidelines on Friday night, they had to make a season long commitment to being at every practice. There was a tremendous correlation between our water boys and the impact on their teams when they became high school age. The great advantage for these boys is that they saw firsthand the work, the discipline, and the intensity needed to succeed as a varsity Mariner. Regardless of their age, the water boys never escaped the wrath of any coach if their practice equipment was not set up correctly, or if the kicking tee was not readily available. They experienced hard coaching at an early age, which helped mold them into motivated and coachable players. The water boys that stick out the most in my memory are the ones that came in packages.

The Osterland twins: Brent and Bryon were easily the most fiery competitors as water boys and later members of the victorious 1996 team that defeated Marysville.

During practice, Denny Fitzsimmons was often targeted for bullying by his older brothers Andrew, Kevin, and Dennis. In turn. All three boys were tough-nosed football players with Kevin being a four-year starter and a captain on the 2013 team.

The Headlee boys: Jared, Jacob, Justin, and Josh were water boy main stays, took the job profoundly serious, and in turn transitioned to some of the hardest hitting Mariners of all time.

The Walker clan: Colby, Mason, and Wyatt—all with vastly unique personalities but who shared the same competitive fire. Colby led his team to the state semifinals in 2018 with Mason and Wyatt being starters on the same team. Wyatt just completed his senior year and led the Mariners back to Ford Field.

The Nelson twins: Ty and Trent—whose uncle is Dave Frendt, our defensive back coach in 2013, and now the Mariner defensive coordinator. Both boys were very smart athletes, and along with Wyatt Walker, contributed to the 2021 return to Ford Field.

Finally, I must talk about the future of Mariner football and my last set of water boys: the Volkman triplets. Tucker, Eli, and Brent were incredibly young when they started with me but were a disciplined and focused group of boys. They came from excellent stock—their parents, David, and Kelly Volkman, were both gifted athletes at Marine City High School. Dave was one of the best running backs we ever produced, as he strung together several 200-yard games in his senior year. Kelly took no crap from anyone in high school and instilled discipline and respect in all five of her kids while looking like she could still compete at a high level. I thoroughly enjoyed any chance I had to sit down and talk with the boys and quite often during warmups of a big game I would deliberately seek them out to take advantage of the calming effect they had on me. All three boys are clearly athletic and understand the game like no one should at their young age. They also have a wonderful sense of humor and many of our conversations ended with, "Good talking with you boys, now get the hell out of here." They would laugh and go back to sideline football...as was the tradition with all our water boys.

The Mariner football program is in good hands. Current head coach, Daryn Letson, has accomplished amazing success in his first three seasons on the job. He led the 2021 team back to Ford Field. Defensive Coordinator, Dave Frendt. is one of the most gifted young coaches I have worked with and continues the great defensive success, which Tony Scarcelli created, and Matt Pollock further established. Position coaches like Andy Scheel, Bill Nesbitt, Jim Heslip, and Dave Osterland have been consummate teachers who *earned* the highest level of respect from the kids. Lower-level coaches like Joe Fregetto, Jason Bell, and Eric Frank set the table for the varsity by putting their egos aside and emphasizing individual improvement over wins and losses. No program can sustain success without excellence from their lower-level coaches, and that is exactly what we have in the Mariner football program.

32

Bring It Home.

At 9:00 a.m. I walked into my dad's hospital room, and he was fully dressed and ready to leave. He stood up immediately and gave me one of the biggest hugs we ever exchanged. One half of me believes the hug stemmed from the championship won the night before, the other half of me believes he was excited to go home and sleep in his own "f**king bed." He struggled to talk, knowing it might lead to prolonged coughing, so I did most of the chit chat and rehashed some moments from the night before. When we got home, he put on his PJ's, and I got a picture of him holding the white championship ball from Ford Field. One hand held the ball around his belly, the other hand had the index finger raised, signaling number one. I never asked Dad to pose like that, and it was out of character from this overly humble man. It is a picture I cherish to this day. I posted the picture on Facebook and let the Mariner faithful know he was home and doing better.

We sat in the living room and watched some college football together, and Dad quickly fell asleep on the couch. It was the same living room where 40 plus years earlier I sat proudly one Christmas morning with my toy helmet, shoulder pads, jersey, and football. My family unit was then, and still is today, incredibly strong. It is the family unit where I learned to celebrate successes but never be afraid to give tough love when needed. It is this family unit that encouraged risk taking and to look at failure as a learning opportunity and a chance for new growth.

One of the magical things Coach Bob did with the Marine City football program was to recreate a strong family unit that started with the coaching staff. His ability to connect with each coach and truly listen to their input and feedback made the process seamless. Coaching meetings in his living room, barbeques on his deck in the summer, and dinner with the wives, created a respect so strong for all the coaches that nobody wanted to let Coach Bob down. As success came to the program, and the coaches remained constant, the teams that followed quickly mirrored the family model. He learned early on that kids in the Marine City community were not afraid of hard work, which is a direct reflection of equally hard-working parents.

The 2013 team consciously or unconsciously took this model to the next level. The captains organized offseason get-togethers and cook-outs. As a group, they jumped into the St. Clair River to cool off after summer workouts. They held each other accountable during film study and in the weight room, and they protected each other on the field of battle. They attacked each challenge the season threw at them, and never blinked when some new challenge raised the bar even higher. The greatest quality they possessed as a team was the concept of PERSISTENCE. In my opinion it is the greatest quality a student/athlete can have. The Mariners of 2013 would not let practice end unless it ended the right way. They would not allow failure to continue on the game field, which led to many heated interactions in the huddle, but no one can argue with the results.

The flow of water in the St. Clair River in the Blue Water area is a constant year in and year out. Water rises and falls in depth each season, but the pace and run of water never varies. The flow of water screams PERSISTENCE to any local resident or any tourist visiting the area. If the Mariner administration continues to see the big picture when hiring teachers and if our coaching staff continues to evolve and improve, the Mariner football program will continue its successful RUN.

Writing this book has made some things crystal clear to me. The first of which is that high school football on a Friday night may be one of the last pieces of America of which we can all be proud. The solidarity in the stands, the field, and in the hearts of the spectators is inspiring. If you need to reset your patriotism or just need your heart and mind to be warmed and motivated, head off to your local high school football game on a Friday night. You might experience the last bastion of a TRUE AMERICA.

DREAM BIG MARINERS,
WORK HARD AND STAY HUMBLE,
AND GREAT THINGS WILL
Flow DOWN YOUR River.

About the Author

RON GLODICH IS not your typical high school football coach. A science teacher by day, his observation skills infiltrate and manifest in his style of coaching.

His induction into the 2018 Michigan Coaches Hall of Fame was well deserved for a young coach who had originated from the cold and dense cement city of Warren, Michigan, to ultimately settle in the beautiful blue-water town of Marine City, Michigan.

In his 33 years working with the Marine City football program, they experienced just one losing season. As head coach in his final eight seasons, Glodich claimed a state championship, five league championships, three district and two regional championships, to go along with a wall full of coaching awards.

Ron Glodich, Author, *A Run to the River*
Published by Silverlight Press
https://www.ronglodich.com/

IN A DIGITAL world, it is difficult to know who has read a book or how well the reader enjoyed it. Short reviews are a gauge of the latter-—and an encouragement to the author to keep writing!

A review is nothing like what we used to have to complete in school! In 25 or more words, you can tell other readers what you liked about the book. Simple and appreciated.